AF695501

THE AI SENSOR ECOSYSTEM

How Artificial Intelligence Sees, Understands, and Connects the World

By

Susie Hala

IntelliGloss Press

Legal Disclaimer

Educational Purpose Disclaimer

"This publication is part of the IntelliGloss AI Education Series, a structured curriculum support system for AI literacy in grades 6–12."

The information presented in this publication is provided for educational and informational purposes only. This book is intended to support educators, administrators, parents, and learners in understanding the concepts, opportunities, and challenges associated with artificial intelligence in education. It is not intended to serve as legal, technical, policy, cybersecurity, or professional advice.

Readers should consult qualified professionals, institutional guidelines, and local regulations before implementing any educational programs, technologies, or policies described in this book.

Technology and Accuracy Disclaimer
Artificial intelligence is a rapidly evolving field. While every effort has been made to ensure the accuracy and reliability of the information presented at the time of publication, technologies, policies, research findings, and best practices may change over time. The author and publisher make no guarantees that all information will remain current or applicable in future technological environments.

Readers are encouraged to verify tools, platforms, and recommendations independently before using them in educational settings.

Implementation Responsibility
Schools, educators, and institutions are solely responsible for determining how and whether to implement artificial intelligence tools, strategies, or classroom activities discussed in this book. Educational environments vary widely, and policies regarding technology use, student privacy, and curriculum development differ by district, state, and country.

The author and publisher assume no responsibility for outcomes resulting from the implementation of ideas, examples, or frameworks described in this book.

Student Safety and Data Privacy
Artificial intelligence tools may involve the collection or processing of data. Educators and institutions are responsible for ensuring that any technology used complies with applicable student privacy laws, data protection regulations, and school policies, including but not limited to FERPA, COPPA, GDPR, or other relevant regulations depending on jurisdiction.

The author and publisher are not responsible for the privacy practices, security policies, or data handling procedures of third-party platforms or software mentioned in this book.

Third-Party Tools and References
This book may reference third-party technologies, organizations, research studies, or platforms for illustrative and educational purposes. Such references do not constitute endorsements or guarantees regarding the performance, reliability, safety, or suitability of those tools for educational use.

Educators and institutions should conduct their own evaluations and risk assessments before adopting any technology.

No Professional Liability
The author and publisher shall not be held liable for any direct, indirect, incidental, or consequential damages resulting from the use or misuse of the information contained in this book. This includes but is not limited to decisions related to curriculum design, technology adoption, classroom instruction, institutional policies, or educational outcomes.

Educational Interpretation
The concepts and examples provided in this book are intended to support discussion and learning. They should not be interpreted as official standards, mandatory guidelines, or universally applicable policies for artificial intelligence education.

Schools and educators are encouraged to adapt the ideas presented here according to their local policies, cultural context, educational standards, and student needs.

Author's Intent
The goal of this book is to promote responsible AI literacy, thoughtful discussion, and ethical awareness as schools prepare students for a world increasingly shaped by intelligent technologies.

The author encourages readers to approach artificial intelligence education with curiosity, caution, and a commitment to responsible learning.

Title: THE AI SENSOR ECOSYSTEM: How Artificial Intelligence Sees, Understands, and Connects the World

ISBN: 978-1-972925-22-5

Copyright © 2026 by Susie Hala
All rights reserved.

No part of this publication may be reproduced, stored in a retrieval system, transmitted, or distributed in any form or by any means—electronic, mechanical, photocopying, recording, or otherwise—without the prior written permission of the author, except in the case of brief quotations used in reviews, educational discussions, or scholarly references.

Published by
IntelliGloss Press
United States of America

This book is intended for educational and informational purposes. Artificial intelligence technologies and policies evolve rapidly, and the author makes no guarantee regarding the completeness, accuracy, or continued applicability of the information presented. Educators, schools, and institutions are responsible for evaluating and implementing technologies in accordance with their own policies, legal requirements, and educational standards.

Unauthorized reproduction of this work may result in legal action.

Dedication

This book is dedicated to the next generation of learners—
the students who will grow up in a world shaped by intelligent technology,
and who deserve to understand it with clarity, confidence, and purpose.

To the educators who show up every day with dedication and heart,
guiding students through a rapidly changing world—
your role has never been more important.

To the parents and families who support learning at home,
encouraging curiosity, responsibility, and growth—
you are the foundation of every child's success.

And to my granddaughters,
whose curiosity, imagination, and future inspire me to do this work—
this book is for you.

May you not only learn how to use technology,
but understand it, question it, and shape it for the good of others.

About the Author

Susie Hala
Founder of the IntelliGloss AI Education Series

Susie Hala is an author, educator, and curriculum developer dedicated to advancing artificial intelligence literacy in education. Her work focuses on helping schools, educators, and students understand how intelligent technologies are shaping modern society—and why that understanding is essential for the next generation.

Hala is the creator of the IntelliGloss AI Education Series, a comprehensive and growing collection of educational books designed to make complex artificial intelligence concepts accessible, structured, and practical for classroom use. Her work emphasizes clarity, organization, and responsible implementation, enabling schools to introduce AI literacy without requiring advanced technical backgrounds.

In addition to her work in education, Hala brings hands-on experience working with artificial intelligence systems, including early exposure to rule-based AI technologies during her time working with AT&T. She has also developed modern digital platforms that integrate artificial intelligence, automation, and online systems, building e-commerce solutions and AI-driven applications that connect payment platforms, hosting environments, and conversational AI tools into real-world, functional systems.

This combination of foundational understanding and practical experience allows her to translate complex AI concepts into clear, accessible language for both educators and students.

Recognizing that artificial intelligence is rapidly transforming how information is created, interpreted, and used, Hala advocates for equipping students with the ability not only to use AI tools, but to understand, question, and evaluate them. Her work emphasizes critical thinking, ethical awareness, and responsible digital citizenship.

The IntelliGloss AI Education Series supports schools in teaching key areas such as artificial intelligence foundations, algorithms, machine learning concepts, and AI ethics, as well as the broader evolution of intelligent systems—from Artificial Narrow Intelligence (ANI) to Artificial General Intelligence (AGI) and Artificial Superintelligence (ASI). These resources are designed for students in grades 6–12 and for educators seeking structured, classroom-ready approaches to AI literacy.

In addition to her work in education publishing, Hala has a strong background in entrepreneurship, having built and managed multiple businesses and educational initiatives. Her experience across industries reinforces her belief that technology education must remain grounded in human values, critical thinking, and ethical responsibility.

Her mission is clear: to ensure that the next generation understands intelligent technology—not just how to use it, but how it truly works.

Preface

Two Students. Two Paths. One Future.

Before we begin, it is important to understand why learning how artificial intelligence works—not just how to use it—matters for every student.

Imagine two students who have just graduated from high school and are preparing for a job interview. The first student knows how to use artificial intelligence tools. This student can generate answers, complete assignments quickly, and rely on AI to assist with tasks. However, this student does not understand how artificial intelligence works behind the scenes.

The second student also knows how to use AI tools, but in addition, understands the foundational concepts behind them. This student has learned about data, algorithms, tokens, models, and how intelligent systems are trained and operate. This student can think critically about AI, recognize its limitations, and adapt when needed.

At first, the first student may appear faster and more efficient. However, over time, the second student demonstrates a deeper level of understanding, independence, and problem-solving ability. The second student is not only able to use artificial intelligence but also to question it, improve it, and grow with it.

This book is written for the second student.

In a world where artificial intelligence is becoming part of everyday life, students must not only learn how to use intelligent systems—they must learn how they work. True understanding leads to confidence, responsibility, and the ability to lead in an AI-driven future.

This perspective is not just theoretical—it is personal.

There was a time when I was the first student.

I knew how to use systems. I followed processes, completed tasks, and worked within structured environments that required accuracy and consistency. At the time, I did not think of these systems as artificial intelligence. They were simply part of the job—tools that had to be learned, followed, and mastered.

But looking back, I now understand something much deeper. I was working within rule-based systems—the earliest foundation of what we now recognize as artificial intelligence.

That realization changed everything.

As I began studying modern AI, including machine learning, deep learning, and intelligent systems, I started to see a clear connection between the past and the present. The structured systems I once worked in, the logic behind decision-making, and the step-by-step processes all still exist today. They have simply evolved.

Artificial intelligence did not appear overnight. It grew from rule-based systems into systems that can now learn, adapt, and assist in ways we never imagined.

I made a decision to move from simply using systems to understanding them.

That journey—from student one to student two—is the reason these books exist.

My mission is to help others bridge that same gap.

I believe that artificial intelligence should be understandable for everyone. It should not feel intimidating or out of reach. Students should feel confident exploring it. Teachers should feel prepared to introduce it. Everyday learners should have access to clear, structured explanations that make sense.

You do not need a background in technology. You do not need to know how to code. You only need the right explanation.

A Note from the Author

AI Is a Tool — Not a Decision Maker

Artificial Intelligence is becoming part of everyday life. Students use it to complete assignments, teachers use it to support instruction, and businesses use it to improve efficiency. While these tools are powerful and useful, there is an important truth that must remain clear from the very beginning:

Artificial Intelligence does not make decisions—people do.

One of the main purposes of this book is to help readers understand how AI works, what it can do, and—just as importantly—what it cannot do. AI systems are designed to process information, identify patterns, and generate responses based on data. They can assist with thinking, but they do not think independently. They can provide answers, but they do not understand consequences. They can suggest ideas, but they do not choose actions.

Every outcome that involves AI begins and ends with human involvement. A person asks the question. A person reviews the response. A person decides what to do next. Responsibility does not transfer to the machine.

In today's world, it is easy to confuse speed with intelligence and automation with authority. Because AI can respond quickly and confidently, it may appear as though it is making decisions. In reality, it is performing a task based on patterns it has learned—not exercising judgment.

This distinction matters. When people begin to rely on AI without understanding its role, they risk misunderstanding information, misusing technology, or placing trust in a system that is not capable of accountability. Clear understanding leads to responsible use.

This book was written to remove confusion and provide clarity. It is designed to help students and educators move beyond simply using AI tools and begin understanding the structure behind them. By learning how AI supports human thinking—rather than replacing it—readers can approach technology with confidence, awareness, and responsibility.

Artificial Intelligence is a powerful assistant. It can enhance learning, support creativity, and improve productivity. But it remains a tool.

The decisions, the actions, and the responsibility will always belong to the human.

— Susie Hala

Bringing Clarity to Artificial Intelligence

During a recent meeting with a school district, it became clear that one of the biggest challenges in artificial intelligence education is not the technology itself—but the way it is explained.

In that discussion, terms such as **chatbots, generative AI, agentic AI, autonomy, tools, hallucinations, and AI usage levels** were all mentioned together. While each term represents a distinct concept, they were often blended into one conversation without clear distinctions. The result was confusion, even among those who were actively trying to understand and make informed decisions.

This experience revealed an important truth:
Without clear definitions and structure, artificial intelligence becomes difficult to teach, difficult to learn, and difficult to use responsibly.

This book is designed to provide that structure.

Understanding the Core Concepts

To build a strong foundation, it is essential to separate and define the key ideas that are often confused.

Chatbot
A chatbot is a conversational interface that allows users to interact with an AI system through questions and prompts. It responds to input but does not act beyond what is directly requested.

Generative AI (Gen AI)
Generative AI refers to systems that create new content, including text, images, audio, and code. These systems generate outputs based on patterns learned from large datasets. While powerful, generative AI does not truly understand information and may occasionally produce inaccurate results.

Agentic AI
Agentic AI describes systems that can take action toward a goal. Rather than responding to a single prompt, these systems can plan, make decisions within defined limits, and carry out multi-step tasks. This introduces a higher level of functional independence.

Autonomy
Autonomy refers to how independently an AI system operates. Some systems require constant human guidance, while others can perform multiple steps with minimal input. Autonomy is not a separate type of AI, but a measure of how much control the system has in completing tasks.

Additional Terms That Shape Understanding

AI Tools
AI tools are the applications people use to interact with artificial intelligence, such as writing assistants, design platforms, and data analysis systems. These tools make AI accessible in everyday tasks.

Hallucination
A hallucination occurs when an AI system generates information that appears correct but is inaccurate or unsupported. This is a known limitation of generative systems and highlights the need for human verification.

The AI Use Continuum

Another important concept is how AI is used at different levels. Rather than viewing AI as a single capability, it is more accurate to understand it as a continuum of use:

Assistive Use
AI supports simple tasks such as answering questions, correcting grammar, or providing suggestions.

Augmented Use
AI helps expand human capability by generating ideas, organizing content, and assisting in problem-solving.

Agentic Use
AI begins to take on multi-step responsibilities, planning and completing tasks with reduced human input.

This continuum shows that AI can range from a helpful assistant to a more independent system, depending on how it is applied.

The Moment Everything Sounded Like One Conversation

During a recent discussion on artificial intelligence, I listened closely as different experts spoke about the future of AI. One referenced advanced systems beyond human intelligence, another discussed goal-driven AI systems, and the conversation shifted quickly between topics like autonomy, tools, and system behavior. At first, it sounded like a single, unified discussion. But the more I listened, the more I realized something important.

They were not all talking about the same thing.

One part of the conversation focused on future possibilities—high-level systems that do not yet exist. Another part focused on current technologies that are already being used today. At the same time, different terms were being used to describe how AI behaves, how it makes decisions, and how much independence it may have. These ideas were layered together in a way that made them sound connected, even when they were not.

This experience revealed a major challenge in understanding artificial intelligence today. Many discussions combine different types of AI, different levels of intelligence, and different behaviors into one conversation. Without clear structure, these ideas begin to blur together. For someone trying to learn, this can feel overwhelming and confusing.

This book is built to solve that problem.

Artificial intelligence is not one single concept. It is a system made up of multiple layers. Some layers describe how intelligent a system is. Other layers describe how the system behaves. Still others describe how much control or independence the system has. When these layers are separated and explained clearly, AI becomes much easier to understand.

The goal of this book is to bring clarity where confusion often exists. Instead of mixing everything into one explanation, each concept is presented in a structured and organized way. This allows students, educators, and readers to see how the pieces fit together without losing sight of what each part actually means.

Understanding artificial intelligence begins with understanding its structure.

Once that structure is clear, the conversation becomes clearer as well.

Why Clarity Matters

When these concepts are not clearly defined, they merge into what can be described as a "conceptual blur." This can lead to misunderstandings about what AI can and cannot do, as well as unrealistic expectations or misuse in educational settings.

Clear understanding helps ensure that:

Students remain active learners, not passive users

Educators maintain control over instructional outcomes

AI is used as a support tool rather than a replacement for thinking

The Purpose of This Book

This book is built on a simple but essential principle:

Students should not only use artificial intelligence—they should understand it.

By clearly defining core concepts such as chatbots, generative AI, agentic AI, autonomy, and the continuum of AI use, this curriculum provides a structured pathway for developing both technical understanding and critical thinking.

Artificial intelligence is not a single tool or system. It is a collection of capabilities that must be understood in context.

Clarity is the foundation of responsible innovation.

Structuring Artificial Intelligence to Create Clarity and Understanding

Why Structure Is Necessary

Artificial intelligence is often presented as one unified concept. In many discussions, different ideas such as intelligence level, system behavior, and autonomy are combined into a single explanation. This can make AI appear more complex and confusing than it actually is.

Clarity begins when these ideas are separated and organized.

Structuring artificial intelligence allows each concept to be understood on its own before being connected to the larger system.

The Problem Without Structure

When AI is not structured, conversations may include multiple terms that sound related but describe entirely different things. For example, a discussion may move quickly between advanced future systems, current tools, and system behaviors without clearly distinguishing between them.

This creates the impression that all forms of AI operate at the same level and in the same way, which is not accurate.

Without structure, understanding becomes difficult.

The Solution: A Structured Approach

Artificial intelligence becomes clearer when it is organized into distinct categories.

Level explains how intelligent a system is.
Behavior explains how the system operates.
Control explains how much independence the system has.

Each category answers a different question. Together, they form a complete picture of how AI systems function.

Clarity Through Separation

A system can operate at a current level of intelligence while demonstrating different behaviors or levels of independence. For example, a system that generates responses and a system that takes steps toward completing a task may operate at the same intelligence level but differ in how they behave.

This distinction becomes clear only when structure is applied.

Instructional Insight

When teaching artificial intelligence, it is important to avoid presenting all concepts at once. Separating ideas into categories allows learners to focus on one dimension at a time, building understanding step by step.

Structured learning leads to deeper comprehension.

Key Takeaway

Artificial intelligence is not one single idea. It is a system made up of multiple parts. Structuring those parts creates clarity, improves understanding, and allows learners to see how the system truly works.

Reflection Question

How does separating intelligence level, behavior, and control make artificial intelligence easier to understand?

The IntelliGloss Instructional Approach

The IntelliGloss AI Education Series is designed to help students move beyond simply using AI tools and begin understanding artificial intelligence as a complete system.

Students learn how AI is built, how it operates, and how it connects to the real world.

A Message to Students and Readers

If you have ever felt that technology was too complicated…
If you have ever been confused by systems that were never clearly explained…

I want you to know:

You are capable of understanding artificial intelligence.

Sometimes, the challenge is not the concept itself—it is how it has been presented.

This series was created to change that.

A Message to Educators

To the educators using this material:

These books are designed to support you in introducing artificial intelligence in a way that is clear, structured, and meaningful for students.

AI is becoming part of every industry, and students deserve more than just exposure to tools—they deserve understanding.

This series aims to provide that foundation.

Final Reflection

Every experience we have—especially the challenging ones—prepares us for something greater.

The systems I once worked in taught me discipline, structure, and attention to detail. Today, those same lessons allow me to break down complex ideas and make them understandable for others.

That is what this series represents:

Turning complexity into clarity.

Why Artificial Intelligence Education Matters for Every Student

Why AI Literacy Is Essential for Every Student

Artificial intelligence is no longer a future concept or a specialized technology used only by experts. It is already part of everyday life for students of all ages. From smartphones and search engines to navigation apps, social media, streaming platforms, and educational tools, AI systems influence how information is accessed, decisions are made, and learning takes place.

Because AI is embedded in daily life, understanding it is no longer optional. It is a foundational skill, similar to digital literacy and critical thinking. Students do not need to become programmers or engineers, but they do need to understand what AI is, how it works at a basic level, and how it affects their lives.

AI education should not be limited to computer science classrooms. Every student interacts with AI systems daily. Teaching students how these systems function empowers them to become informed users rather than passive consumers of technology.

This book is designed to make artificial intelligence understandable, approachable, and relevant. It focuses on clarity, responsibility, and real-world understanding to help students prepare for a future where humans and intelligent systems work side by side.

IntelliGloss AI Education Series

Teaching how AI actually works—from hardware to power to global systems.

Why AI Education Matters

Artificial intelligence is already shaping how students learn, write, research, and solve problems.

Yet many students—and educators—are using AI tools without understanding how these systems actually work.

Schools need more than access to technology.
They need structured, responsible AI education.

Our Approach

The IntelliGloss AI Education Series is designed to help students move beyond simply using AI tools and begin understanding artificial intelligence as a complete system.

Students learn how AI is built, how it operates, and how it connects to the real world.

The IntelliGloss Framework

Our books introduce AI through a clear and connected system:

Chip Family — the hardware that powers AI

Watts Family — the rate at which AI uses power

Energy Family — the total power AI consumes over time

Infrastructure Family — the global systems that support AI

This framework helps students understand AI from the inside out.

Built for the Classroom

Each book includes:

Structured chapters aligned with semester learning

Clear explanations designed for student understanding

Reflection sections with learning objectives

Worksheets, quizzes, and answer keys

Teacher Implementation Guides

Supporting Schools and Educators

The IntelliGloss series supports:

Responsible and ethical AI use

Student data awareness and safety

Critical thinking and digital literacy

Classroom-ready instruction for grades 6–12 and beyond

What This Book Is—and What It Is Not

Many people today are becoming familiar with artificial intelligence through tools like ChatGPT, Microsoft Copilot, Canva, and other AI-powered applications. These tools can help with writing, answering questions, creating images, and completing everyday tasks.

In addition to these tools, you may also hear terms such as **AI agents, agentic AI, autonomous systems, and generative AI**. While these may sound complex, they are all part of the same evolving landscape of artificial intelligence technologies.

This book is not a guide on how to use those tools.

Instead, it explains what makes those tools possible.

Behind every AI tool is a system made up of multiple layers working together. At the most basic level, information is represented as bits and processed through powerful computer chips. That information is organized into data, broken into tokens, and then processed by algorithms and models that allow the system to recognize patterns, generate responses, and perform tasks.

These components—chips, bits, tokens, data, algorithms, and models—work together as a complete system. While users may only see the tool, the real intelligence comes from how these underlying parts interact behind the scenes.

Artificial intelligence can also be understood in terms of different levels of capability. Most of the AI systems used today fall under **Artificial Narrow Intelligence (ANI)**, which is designed to perform specific tasks, such as answering questions or generating content. More advanced forms, such as **Artificial General Intelligence (AGI)** and **Artificial Superintelligence (ASI)** represent future possibilities where AI could match or exceed human-level thinking. While these advanced levels are still theoretical, understanding the differences helps provide a broader view of where AI is today and where it may be heading.

For students, parents, and educators, this distinction is important. Learning how to use AI tools is helpful, but understanding how they work—and where they fit within the larger AI landscape—builds stronger thinking, better decision-making, and more responsible use.

Most importantly, artificial intelligence does not make decisions on its own. It does not take responsibility for actions or outcomes. AI systems generate responses based on data and patterns, but it is always the human who decides what to do with that information.

This book is designed to make these underlying systems clear and accessible, even for readers who are new to artificial intelligence.

Artificial intelligence is still in its early stages of development. As these technologies continue to grow, those who understand the foundation behind them will be better prepared to adapt, question, and use them wisely.

Who This Book Is For

This book is designed for educators, school leaders, and curriculum developers guiding students in an age of rapidly advancing technology.

Artificial intelligence is already influencing how students learn, research, and communicate. Yet many educators have not received formal training in how these systems work or how they should be addressed in the classroom.

This book helps bridge that gap by providing clear explanations and practical frameworks for understanding artificial intelligence in an educational setting.

How Schools Can Use This Book

This book supports schools in developing a structured approach to artificial intelligence literacy.

It can be used for:

Professional development for educators

Classroom discussions and activities

Curriculum support across subject areas

Policy and academic integrity conversations

Rather than focusing on specific tools, this book emphasizes lasting principles that help students understand, evaluate, and use AI responsibly.

Closing Perspective

Artificial intelligence will continue to evolve. With the right knowledge and leadership, schools can ensure that students not only use these technologies, but understand them, question them, and apply them responsibly.

IntelliGloss is more than a book series. It is a structured approach to preparing students for a future shaped by artificial intelligence.

Rather than focusing only on how to use AI tools, this series helps students understand how AI actually works—from its foundational building blocks to real-world applications.

"Before exploring the technical structure of artificial intelligence, it is equally important to understand the human principles that guide its use."

Human Values Family

Definition

The Human Values Family in artificial intelligence represents the guiding principles that shape how AI systems are created, used, and integrated into society. These values include ethics, responsibility, trust, and human well-being.

Artificial intelligence may be built on data, algorithms, and computational systems, but its true impact is measured by how it affects people. For this reason, AI is not only a technical system—it is a human-centered system.

Key Concepts

The Human Values Family exists to ensure that artificial intelligence serves humanity in a positive and responsible way. While AI systems can process information and generate outcomes, they do not possess judgment, empathy, or moral understanding.

This means that human values must guide every stage of AI development—from design to deployment.

AI reflects the intentions, decisions, and assumptions of the people who build and use it. If those values are not carefully considered, AI systems can unintentionally produce biased, harmful, or misleading results.

Understanding human values in AI is not optional—it is essential.

Core Elements of the Human Values Family

Ethics

Ethics in AI refers to making decisions that are fair, just, and respectful of human rights. This includes minimizing bias, protecting privacy, and ensuring transparency in how systems operate.

Responsibility

Responsibility means that humans remain accountable for AI systems. Developers, educators, organizations, and users must take ownership of how AI is used and the outcomes it produces.

Trust

Trust is critical for the successful adoption of AI. People must feel confident that AI systems are reliable, safe, and aligned with their best interests.

Human Well-Being

AI should enhance human life—not replace, harm, or diminish it. This includes supporting learning, improving access to information, and creating opportunities while maintaining human dignity.

Real-World Connection

Artificial intelligence is already influencing how people learn, communicate, and make decisions. From search engines to classroom tools, AI is shaping daily experiences.

Without clear human values guiding these systems, there is a risk of reinforcing misinformation, bias, or unrealistic expectations.

For students, this means learning not only how to use AI tools, but how to question them, evaluate their outputs, and understand their limitations.

Applications in Education

In the classroom, the Human Values Family helps students develop critical thinking and ethical awareness. Teachers can use this framework to guide discussions about fairness, responsibility, and the impact of technology on society.

Students can explore questions such as:

How should AI be used responsibly?

What makes an AI system fair?

How does technology influence human behavior?

This approach supports both technical understanding and responsible decision-making.

Benefits

Teaching human values in AI helps students:

Develop ethical awareness

Strengthen critical thinking

Understand the societal impact of technology

Become responsible users and future creators of AI

It ensures that learning about AI goes beyond functionality and includes responsibility.

Challenges

Human values are not always universal. Different cultures, communities, and individuals may have different perspectives on what is considered fair or ethical.

Additionally, AI technology is evolving rapidly, often faster than policies and guidelines can keep up. This makes it essential for educators and students to stay informed and adaptable.

Summary

The Human Values Family reminds us that artificial intelligence is not just about machines—it is about people.

By focusing on ethics, responsibility, trust, and human well-being, students can learn to use AI thoughtfully and responsibly.

Understanding these principles helps prepare learners to navigate a world where artificial intelligence plays an increasingly important role in everyday life.

Executive Summary

IntelliGloss AI Education Series

Teaching How Artificial Intelligence Actually Works

Artificial intelligence is already shaping how students learn, write, research, and make decisions. Yet in many classrooms, students are being introduced to AI tools without understanding how these systems actually function.

This creates a critical gap.

Students may become efficient users of technology, but without foundational knowledge, they are not equipped to think critically, evaluate outputs, or use AI responsibly. As AI continues to expand across every industry, this gap will only grow more significant.

The **IntelliGloss AI Education Series** was created to address this challenge.

The Problem

Most current approaches to AI in education focus on tool usage rather than system understanding. As a result:

Students rely on AI without understanding its limitations

Educators lack structured frameworks for teaching AI concepts

Key terms such as generative AI, agentic AI, and autonomy are often introduced without clear definitions

Responsibility and ethical use are not consistently emphasized

Without clarity, artificial intelligence becomes difficult to teach, difficult to learn, and difficult to manage in a school environment.

The Solution

The IntelliGloss AI Education Series provides a structured, classroom-ready approach to artificial intelligence literacy for grades 6–12.

Rather than focusing on individual tools, this series teaches students how AI works as a complete system—from foundational components to real-world applications.

Students learn to move beyond surface-level interaction and develop true understanding.

The IntelliGloss Framework

The series introduces AI through a clear and connected structure, including:

Foundational building blocks such as data, algorithms, tokens, and models

System-level understanding through categories such as intelligence level, behavior, and control

Real-world context through applications, limitations, and responsible use

Human-centered learning through ethics, responsibility, trust, and student safety

This structured approach transforms artificial intelligence from a confusing concept into an understandable system.

Instructional Design

Each book in the series is designed for practical classroom use and includes:

Structured chapters aligned with instructional pacing

Clear, student-friendly explanations

Reflection sections to reinforce understanding

Worksheets, quizzes, and answer keys

Teacher implementation support

No prior technical background is required for educators or students.

Guiding Principle

A central message of the IntelliGloss series is:

Artificial Intelligence is a tool—not a decision maker.

Students learn that while AI can support thinking and provide information, all decisions, actions, and responsibilities remain with humans. This principle reinforces critical thinking, accountability, and responsible technology use.

Why It Matters

AI literacy is no longer optional. It is a foundational skill.

Students who understand how AI works will be better prepared to:

Think critically about information

Adapt to emerging technologies

Use AI responsibly and ethically

Succeed in an increasingly AI-driven world

Our Goal

The IntelliGloss AI Education Series is designed to help schools move beyond simply using artificial intelligence tools and toward a deeper understanding of how these systems actually work.

By providing clear structure, defined concepts, and real-world context, this series equips students and educators with the knowledge needed to think critically, evaluate information, and use AI responsibly.

The goal is not just to introduce technology—but to build understanding, confidence, and accountability in an AI-driven world.

This is not just about learning to use AI—it is about preparing students to understand it, question it, and lead with it.

**Clarity leads to confidence.
Understanding leads to responsible use.**

Mission Statement

The mission of the IntelliGloss AI Education Series is to make artificial intelligence clear, structured, and accessible for every student and educator.

In a world where AI is rapidly transforming how information is created, used, and understood, this series is designed to move beyond surface-level interaction and provide a deeper understanding of how intelligent systems actually work.

Through clear explanations, organized frameworks, and real-world context, IntelliGloss equips learners with the ability to think critically, evaluate information, and engage with technology responsibly.

This mission is grounded in a simple belief:
students should not only learn how to use artificial intelligence—they should understand it.

By building both technical awareness and human-centered understanding, the IntelliGloss AI Education Series prepares students to navigate, question, and shape a future increasingly influenced by intelligent technologies.

The goal is not just to keep up with artificial intelligence—but to understand it, guide it, and use it responsibly.

Vision Statement

The vision of the IntelliGloss AI Education Series is to create a future where artificial intelligence is clearly understood, responsibly used, and thoughtfully integrated into education and everyday life.

In this future, students are not passive users of technology, but informed thinkers who understand how intelligent systems work, recognize their limitations, and apply them with purpose and responsibility.

Educators are equipped with clear frameworks and structured resources that make artificial intelligence accessible, teachable, and meaningful across all subjects—not just in technical fields.

Schools become environments where technology is not simply adopted, but understood—where students are encouraged to question, evaluate, and engage with AI in ways that support learning, creativity, and ethical awareness.

As artificial intelligence continues to evolve, this vision supports a generation that is prepared not only to adapt to change, but to lead it with knowledge, confidence, and integrity.

The future of artificial intelligence will not be defined by technology alone—but by the understanding and responsibility of those who use it.

Connecting AI Understanding to Cybersecurity Awareness

Definition

Understanding artificial intelligence is the first step toward understanding cybersecurity. While cybersecurity focuses on protecting systems, data, and users, artificial intelligence explains how those systems are built, how they function, and where they may be vulnerable.

The Connection

Every AI system is made up of components such as data, algorithms, models, and infrastructure. These same components are also the targets of cybersecurity threats.

When students understand:

- How data is collected and stored
- How algorithms make decisions
- How AI models process information
- How systems operate across frontend and backend layers

They begin to recognize where risks can exist and how systems can be misused.

Why This Matters

In today's digital world, students are not just users of technology—they are participants in complex systems powered by artificial intelligence.

Without understanding how these systems work:

- Technology becomes something they trust without question
- Risks become harder to recognize

Decisions are made without awareness of consequences

With understanding:

Students become more aware of how their data is used

They recognize how systems can be manipulated

They make more informed and responsible choices

Building Digital Readiness

Digital readiness is not only about using tools. It is about understanding the systems behind those tools.

By learning how AI works, students develop:

Awareness of digital environments

Confidence in navigating technology

A foundation for future learning, including cybersecurity

Conclusion

Cybersecurity begins with understanding.

Before students can protect systems, they must first understand how those systems are built and how they operate. This is why learning artificial intelligence is not only about innovation—it is also about responsibility.

The Foundation of Artificial Intelligence

Definition

The foundation of Artificial Intelligence (AI) refers to the core building blocks that allow AI systems to function. These building blocks work together to help machines learn from information, recognize patterns, and make decisions. AI is not magic—it is a system built on structured components that operate behind the scenes.

Understanding the Foundation in Simple Terms

Artificial Intelligence can be compared to a house. Before a house is complete, it must be built on a strong foundation. This foundation includes concrete, wiring, plumbing, and support structures that are not always visible but are essential for the house to function properly.

In the same way, AI systems rely on foundational components that are not visible to users but are necessary for AI tools to work. When people use AI applications such as chatbots or design tools, they are interacting with the surface. The true power of AI comes from what is underneath.

Key Components of the AI Foundation

1. Data (The Information)

Data is the starting point of all AI systems. It includes text, images, numbers, audio, and other forms of information. AI systems learn by analyzing patterns within this data.

2. Algorithms (The Instructions)

Algorithms are step-by-step instructions that tell the AI system how to process data. They guide how the system learns, identifies patterns, and produces results.

3. Models (The Trained System)

A model is created when data and algorithms are combined through a training process. The model acts as the "brain" of the AI system, allowing it to make predictions and generate responses.

4. Computing Power (The Engine)

AI systems require powerful computers to process large amounts of data. This includes specialized hardware such as processors and graphics processing units (GPUs) that allow AI to function efficiently.

5. Infrastructure (The Environment)

Infrastructure refers to the systems that support AI operations, including servers, storage, networks, and energy systems. Data centers are a key part of this infrastructure, providing the physical space where AI systems operate.

How These Components Work Together

AI systems function by combining all foundational components into a single process. Data is collected and analyzed using algorithms. This process creates a model that can recognize patterns and make decisions. The entire system is powered by computing machines and supported by infrastructure.

Why Understanding the Foundation Matters

Many people use AI tools without understanding how they work. This can lead to confusion, misuse, or over-reliance on technology. By understanding the foundation of AI, students and educators can:

Develop critical thinking skills

Use AI tools more responsibly

Recognize the limitations of AI systems

Build a deeper understanding of modern technology

Real-World Example

When a student asks a chatbot a question, the response does not come from "thinking" like a human. Instead, the AI system uses a trained model that has learned patterns from large amounts of data. It follows algorithms to predict the most appropriate answer, using powerful computers and infrastructure to deliver the response quickly.

This process is also influenced by how the question is asked. The words, structure, and clarity of a question—often referred to as a *prompt*—can affect the quality of the response. Learning how to communicate effectively with AI systems is an important skill known as prompt engineering. For further understanding, students and educators may explore *What to Say When You Talk to Yourself: A Guide to Prompt Engineering* by Susie Hala, which explains how carefully structured prompts can guide AI responses more effectively.

Conclusion

The foundation of Artificial Intelligence is built on data, algorithms, models, computing power, and infrastructure. These components work together to create systems that can learn, predict, and assist humans. Understanding this foundation helps students move beyond simply using AI tools and toward truly understanding how artificial intelligence works.

The Foundational Families of Artificial Intelligence

Introduction

Artificial intelligence is often described as a powerful technology, but in reality, it is not a single system. It is a combination of multiple components working together to create intelligent behavior.

To better understand how artificial intelligence works, it is helpful to break it down into organized groups. In the IntelliGloss framework, these groups are called **Foundational Families of Artificial Intelligence**.

Each family represents a key part of how AI systems are built and operate. Some families focus on how information is created and stored. Others focus on how machines learn, make decisions, process language, or perform tasks. Additional families represent the physical hardware, energy systems, and global infrastructure that make artificial intelligence possible.

When these families work together, they form a complete AI system.

This approach allows students and educators to move beyond simply using artificial intelligence tools and begin to understand what is happening behind the scenes. Instead of viewing AI as a mystery, learners can see it as a structured system made up of clearly defined components.

The diagram on the next page provides a visual overview of these families and how they connect to form the foundation of artificial intelligence.

By learning each family step by step, students develop a deeper understanding of how AI systems process information, learn from data, and interact with the world.

Understanding the Foundational Families of Artificial Intelligence is the first step toward true AI literacy.

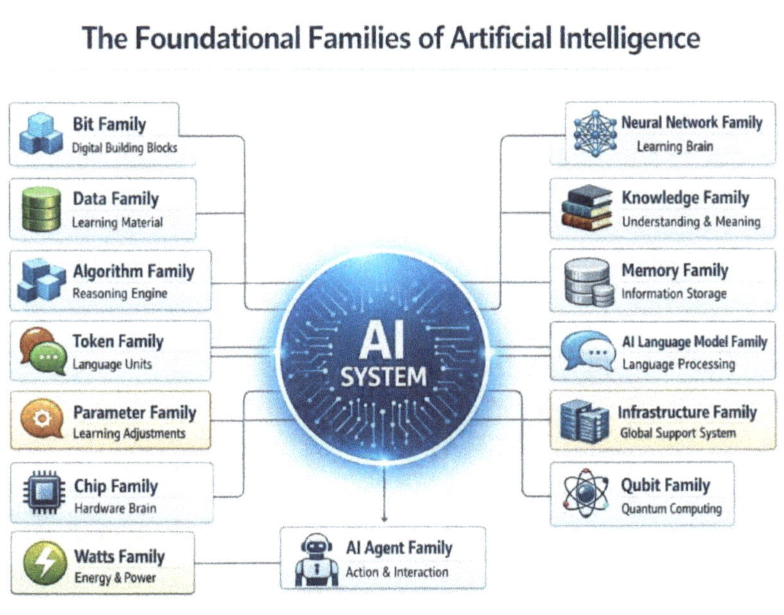

The Foundational Families of Artificial Intelligence

Family	Role	Description
Bit Family	Digital Building Blocks	The smallest unit of digital information (0 or 1). All computing systems begin with bits.
Algorithm Family	Reasoning Engine	Step-by-step instructions that tell computers how to solve problems and process information.
Token Family	Language Units	Pieces of text used by AI models to understand and generate human language.
Parameter Family	Learning Adjustment System	Adjustable numerical values inside AI models that allow them to learn patterns from data.
Data Family	Learning Material	The information AI studies in order to learn patterns, relationships, and knowledge.
Logic Family	Decision Rules	The reasoning structures that allow AI systems to make decisions and evaluate conditions.
Memory Family	Information Storage	Systems that store and retrieve information so AI models can access past knowledge and context.
Knowledge Family	Understanding & Meaning	Structured information that allows AI to represent facts, relationships, and concepts.
Neural Network Family	Learning Brain	Interconnected layers of artificial neurons that enable AI systems to recognize patterns, learn from data, and make predictions.
AI Model Family	Intelligence Engine	The trained system that uses data, parameters, and neural networks to perform tasks such as prediction, classification, and generation.
AI Translator Architecture Family	Language Conversion System	Systems that transform input into output, enabling AI to convert text, speech, or images into meaningful responses.
AI Agent Family	Action and Task Execution System	AI systems designed to perceive information, make decisions, and carry out tasks autonomously or semi-autonomously.
Chip Family	Hardware Brain	Physical processors (GPUs, TPUs, CPUs, NPUs) that perform AI computations.
Watts Family	Energy Power	The electrical power required to run AI hardware and data centers.
AI Energy Family	Energy Source System	The total energy consumed over time to operate AI systems, including training and real-time usage.
Infrastructure Family	Global Support System	Data centers, internet networks, cloud systems, and global infrastructure that allow AI to operate and scale.

Family	Role	Description
Ingredient Family	System Composition	The essential components that come together to create an AI system, including data, algorithms, models, hardware, and energy.
Qubit Family	Quantum Information Units	Quantum bits that can represent multiple states simultaneously, forming the foundation of quantum computing.

The Bit Family

Introduction

The Bit Family represents the starting point of all digital technology. Every computer system, application, and artificial intelligence model is built from bits—the smallest unit of information in computing.

A bit can hold one of two values: 0 or 1. While this may seem simple, these two values form the foundation of everything digital. When bits are combined and organized, they create larger units of data that allow computers to store text, display images, play videos, and run complex systems.

From a single bit to massive data systems, all digital information follows this same structure. This is how computers are able to represent and process the world in a form they can understand.

In artificial intelligence, bits are essential because they store the data that models learn from, process the calculations that drive decision-making, and support the systems that generate responses.

Understanding the Bit Family helps students see how simple binary signals grow into powerful technologies. It reveals that behind every advanced AI system is a foundation built from the most basic building blocks of information.

Bit Family — Visual Understanding of Data Size

How Much Data Can Each Unit Hold? (Simple Examples)

Unit	Size	Photos (Approx.)	Video (Approx. Hours)
Bit	1 bit	N/A	N/A
Byte	8 bits	1 character	N/A
Kilobyte (KB)	~1,000 bytes	Part of a paragraph	N/A
Megabyte (MB)	~1,000 KB	~1 photo	~1 minute of video
Gigabyte (GB)	~1,000 MB	~250 photos	~1–2 hours of video
Terabyte (TB)	~1,000 GB	~250,000 photos	~1,000–2,000 hours of video
Petabyte (PB)	~1,000 TB	~250 million photos	~1–2 million hours of video

Unit	Size	Photos (Approx.)	Video (Approx. Hours)
Exabyte (EB)	~1,000 PB	~250 billion photos	~1–2 billion hours of video
Zettabyte (ZB)	~1,000 EB	~250 trillion photos	~1–2 trillion hours of video
Yottabyte (YB)	~1,000 ZB	~250 quadrillion photos	~1–2 quadrillion hours of video

---

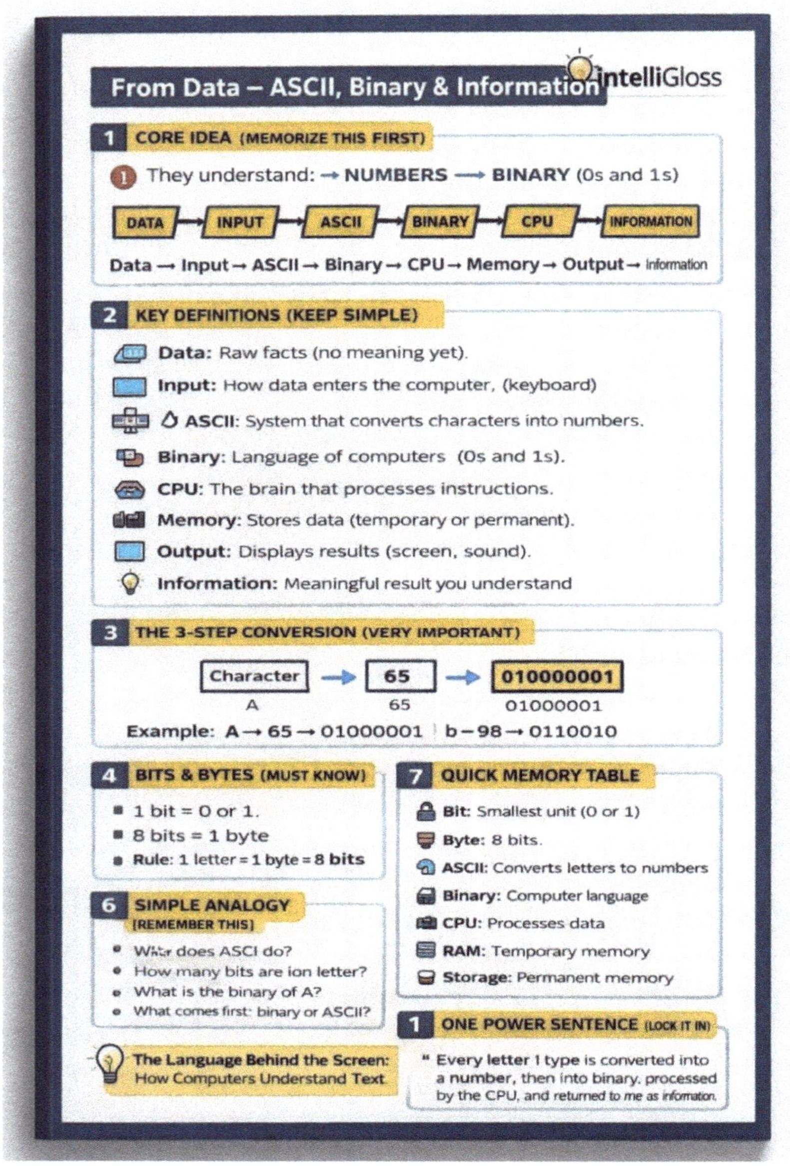

The Algorithm Family

Definition and Overview

The **Algorithm Family** represents the *thinking engine* of artificial intelligence — the set of mathematical instructions that guide how AI analyzes data, learns patterns, and makes decisions.

An **algorithm** is a sequence of steps designed to solve a problem or complete a task. In AI, algorithms tell the system *how to learn*, *how to predict*, and *how to improve* with every iteration.

In simple terms:

The Algorithm Family is the *logic of intelligence* — the invisible code that transforms data into decisions and predictions into progress.

How Algorithms Power AI

Every AI system — from simple chatbots to large-scale deep learning models — relies on algorithms as its foundation.
They determine how the model:

- Processes and cleans data,
- Identifies relationships between variables,
- Learns from feedback, and
- Improves over time.

Without algorithms, even the most powerful dataset or neural network would remain static and lifeless.

In essence, **algorithms are the teachers** that train AI how to think.

Why the Algorithm Family Matters

Algorithms are what separate automation from intelligence.
They allow machines to **reason**, **adapt**, and **learn** — not just follow commands.
For prompt engineers, understanding algorithmic behavior helps explain *why* AI sometimes misunderstands a question, repeats patterns, or changes tone after feedback.

Every AI response you receive follows an underlying process — a pattern recognition journey from input to output.

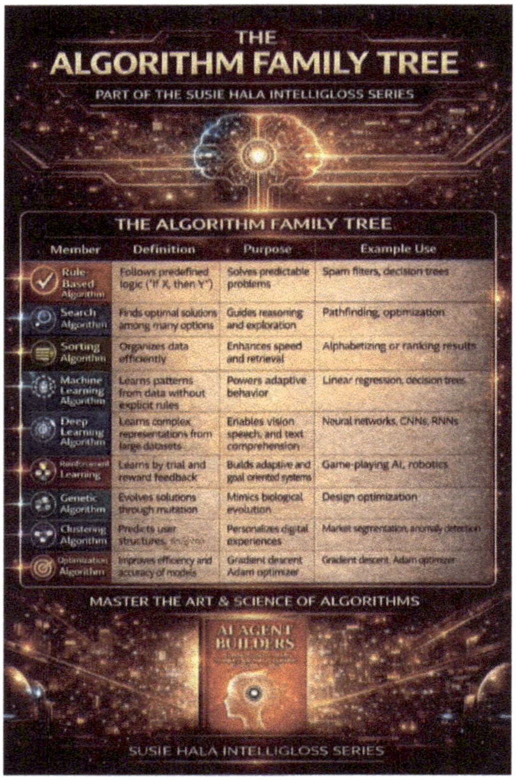

Analogy for Everyday Readers

Imagine AI as a chef in a kitchen:

The **Data Family** provides the ingredients.

The **Knowledge Family** gives the recipes.

The **Algorithm Family** is the *cooking process* — mixing, heating, tasting, and adjusting until the dish is perfect.

Just as cooking methods determine the quality of food, algorithms determine the quality of intelligence.

Algorithm Efficiency and Energy Use

Not all algorithms are equal.
Some are **fast but shallow**, while others are **deep but energy-intensive**.
Training large AI models requires algorithms that can handle billions of calculations per second — powered by the **Watts Family** (energy) and executed through the **Chip Family** (hardware).

The design of efficient algorithms directly affects sustainability in AI — minimizing power consumption while maximizing accuracy and speed.

Algorithms and Prompt Engineering

For prompt engineers, algorithms explain *how* the AI arrives at its answers.
When a model gives inconsistent or off-topic results, it's often due to:

Misinterpretation of input signals (input encoding),

Bias in training algorithms, or

Overfitting to certain data patterns.

Knowing this helps you craft prompts that guide the AI's decision-making — not just its output.

Quick Takeaway: The Algorithm Family is the reasoning heart of AI.
It transforms information into understanding and enables machines to think, learn, and evolve like digital problem-solvers.

Token Family Introduction

The Token Family represents one of the most important bridges between human language and artificial intelligence. While humans communicate using words, sentences, and meaning, AI systems do not understand language in the same way. Instead, they rely on tokens—small units of text that allow machines to process, analyze, and generate language step by step.

A token can be a word, part of a word, a character, or even punctuation. When a student types a sentence into an AI system, that sentence is not read as a whole idea. It is first broken down into tokens. These tokens become the input that the AI model uses to recognize patterns, predict outcomes, and generate responses.

The Token Family works closely with several other foundational families in artificial intelligence. It connects directly with the Data Family, which provides the text used for training, and the Neural Network Family, which processes token patterns to produce intelligent outputs. It also plays a key role in the AI Translator Architecture Family, where tokens are transformed, analyzed, and reassembled into meaningful responses.

Understanding tokens helps students see what is happening behind the scenes when they interact with AI tools. Instead of viewing AI as a "magic system," they begin to understand that every response is built from sequences of tokens processed through mathematical models.

In simple terms, if language is what humans speak, tokens are what AI understands.

Token Family Breakdown Chart

Component	Role	Description	Example
Tokenization	Input Conversion	The process of breaking text into smaller units (tokens) that AI can process	"Artificial Intelligence" → "Artificial" + "Intelligence"
Tokens	Language Units	The individual pieces of text used by AI models for understanding and generation	"AI", "learn", "ing", "."
Subword Tokens	Efficiency Units	Words split into smaller parts to handle unknown or complex vocabulary	"unbelievable" → "un", "believ", "able"
Character Tokens	Fine-Grained Units	Text broken down into individual characters for detailed processing	"AI" → "A" + "I"
Vocabulary (Token Set)	Token Library	The complete set of tokens an AI model recognizes and uses	GPT models have thousands to millions of tokens
Encoding	Token Mapping	Converting tokens into numerical representations for computation	"AI" → [1234, 5678] (example IDs)
Decoding	Output Reconstruction	Converting numerical outputs back into readable text	[1234, 5678] → "AI system"
Context Window	Memory Limit	The number of tokens an AI can process at one time	Example: 8,000 tokens ≈ several pages of text
Token Embeddings	Meaning Representation	Mathematical vectors that capture relationships between tokens	"king" and "queen" have similar embeddings
Token Prediction	Language Generation	The process of predicting the next token in a sequence	"AI is" → predicts "powerful"

The Token Family reminds us that behind every intelligent response is a structured sequence of tokens working together. What feels like natural conversation to humans is, for AI, a carefully processed stream of language units transformed into meaning.

The AI Ecosystem Family

The AI Ecosystem Family is a connected group of artificial intelligence technologies, systems, behaviors, and applications that work together to help machines perform intelligent tasks. This ecosystem includes core AI systems, AI agents, agentic AI, AI autonomy, autonomous AI workers, and generative AI. Each part plays a different role in how modern AI systems think, learn, create, make decisions, solve problems, and interact with the world.

At the center of the ecosystem is artificial intelligence itself — the broad field focused on building machines and software that can perform tasks that normally require human intelligence. AI agents act as the systems that carry out goals and actions. Agentic AI describes the ability of

AI systems to plan, reason, adapt, and pursue objectives with limited human guidance. AI autonomy represents the level of independence an AI system has while making decisions and taking actions. AI autonomous workers apply these capabilities to perform real-world tasks like digital employees or assistants. Generative AI adds the ability to create new content such as text, images, music, video, code, and designs.

The AI Ecosystem Family demonstrates that modern artificial intelligence is no longer just one single technology. Instead, it is an interconnected environment of systems, tools, intelligence, automation, creativity, and human collaboration. As AI continues to evolve, these technologies are becoming increasingly integrated into education, business, healthcare, communication, cybersecurity, research, and everyday life.

Understanding the AI Ecosystem Family helps students, educators, and readers see how the different parts of AI connect together to shape the future of intelligent systems and the digital world.

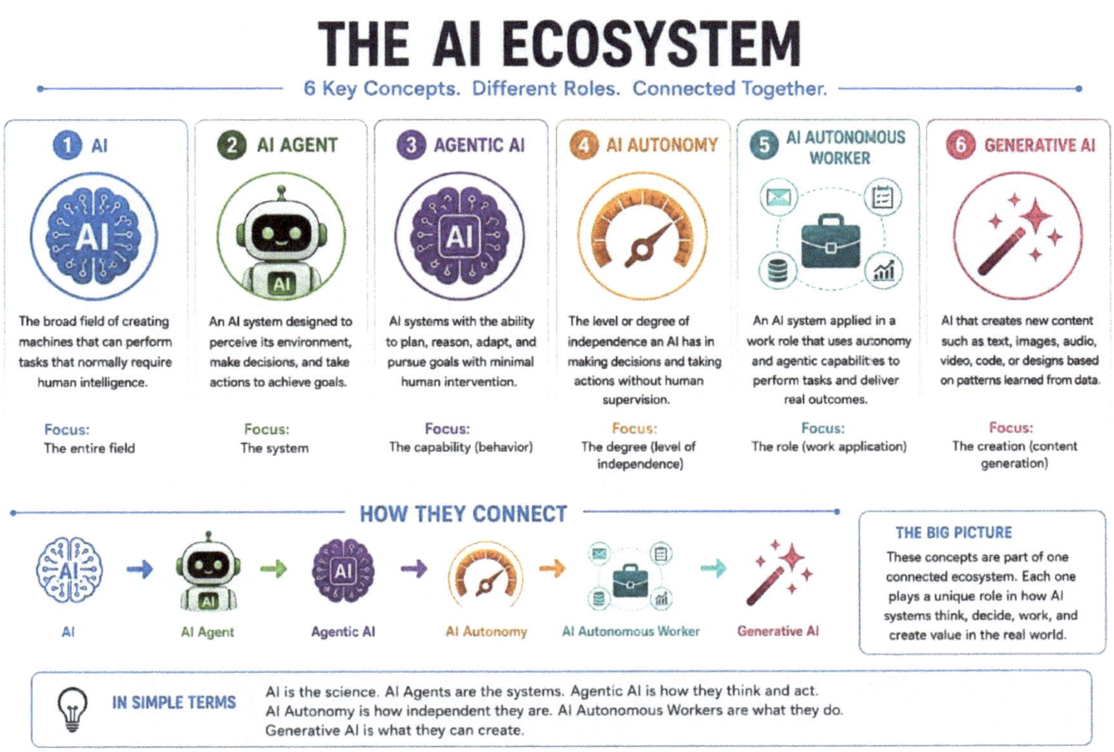

Parameter Family Introduction

The Parameter Family represents the internal learning system of artificial intelligence. While tokens provide the language and data provides the learning material, parameters are what allow AI systems to adjust, improve, and make intelligent decisions over time.

In simple terms, parameters are numerical values inside an AI model that change as the system learns. These values are not visible to users, but they play a critical role in how the model understands patterns, relationships, and meaning. Every time an AI system is trained, it adjusts its parameters to better predict outcomes and generate accurate responses.

Parameters exist throughout neural networks, where they act as the connections between artificial neurons. Each connection has a weight, which determines how important a particular piece of information is. During training, these weights are continuously adjusted based on data, allowing the system to improve its performance.

The Parameter Family works closely with the Data Family, which provides the information needed for learning, and the Neural Network Family, which organizes how parameters are structured and applied. It also supports the Token Family by helping the model interpret and predict sequences of language.

Understanding parameters helps students recognize that AI is not simply programmed with fixed rules. Instead, it learns by adjusting internal values that guide how it processes information. These adjustments are what allow AI systems to evolve from simple pattern recognition to complex reasoning and decision-making.

In essence, if data is what AI learns from, parameters are how AI learns.

Parameter Family Breakdown Chart

Component	Role	Description	Example
Parameters	Learning Values	Numerical values inside an AI model that are adjusted during training	Millions or billions of values inside a model
Weights	Connection Strength	Values that determine how strongly one neuron influences another	A higher weight = stronger influence
Bias	Adjustment Factor	A value added to help the model shift and fine-tune outputs	Helps improve accuracy in predictions
Training Process	Learning Mechanism	The process of adjusting parameters using data to improve performance	Model improves after analyzing many examples

Component	Role	Description	Example
Loss Function	Error Measurement	Measures how far the model's prediction is from the correct answer	Lower loss = better performance
Optimization Algorithm	Adjustment Strategy	Method used to update parameters efficiently	Gradient Descent adjusts weights step by step
Gradient	Direction of Change	Indicates how parameters should change to reduce error	Shows whether to increase or decrease a value
Backpropagation	Learning Process	System that sends error signals backward to update parameters	Adjusts earlier layers based on output error
Hyperparameters	Control Settings	External settings that guide how training happens (not learned)	Learning rate, batch size
Model Size	Capacity Indicator	The total number of parameters in a model	Larger models = more learning capacity

The Parameter Family is the hidden engine of learning in artificial intelligence. While users interact with outputs, it is the continuous adjustment of parameters behind the scenes that makes intelligent behavior possible.

Data Family Introduction

The Data Family represents the foundation of learning in artificial intelligence. Every AI system depends on data to develop knowledge, recognize patterns, and make decisions. Without data, artificial intelligence cannot learn, adapt, or function effectively.

Data can take many forms, including text, images, audio, video, and numerical information. These inputs provide the raw material that AI systems analyze during training. By studying large amounts of data, AI models begin to identify patterns, relationships, and structures that allow them to make predictions and generate responses.

The quality and diversity of data play a critical role in how well an AI system performs. Accurate, balanced, and relevant data helps models produce reliable results, while poor or biased data can lead to incorrect or unfair outcomes. This is why data collection, preparation, and evaluation are essential steps in the development of responsible AI systems.

The Data Family works closely with the Parameter Family, which adjusts internal values based on data, and the Neural Network Family, which processes and organizes data through layers of computation. It also supports the Token Family when dealing with language, as text data is converted into tokens for analysis.

Understanding the Data Family helps students recognize that AI does not "know" things on its own. Instead, it learns from the information it is given. The more meaningful and well-prepared the data, the more capable the AI system becomes.

In simple terms, data is the source of knowledge, and it is the starting point for all artificial intelligence.

Data Family Breakdown Chart

Component	Role	Description	Example
Data	Learning Material	Raw information used by AI systems to learn patterns and relationships	Text, images, audio, numbers
Dataset	Organized Collection	A structured group of data used for training and evaluation	A folder of labeled images
Training Data	Learning Input	Data used to teach the AI model during training	Thousands of sentences for a language model
Validation Data	Performance Check	Data used to tune the model during training without directly learning from it	Helps prevent overfitting
Test Data	Final Evaluation	Data used to measure how well the model performs after training	New unseen examples
Structured Data	Organized Format	Data arranged in tables with clear categories	Spreadsheets, databases
Unstructured Data	Flexible Format	Data without a predefined structure	Text documents, images, videos
Labeled Data	Guided Learning	Data tagged with correct answers to guide training	Image labeled "cat" or "dog"
Unlabeled Data	Self-Learning Input	Data without labels, used in unsupervised learning	Raw text without categories
Data Quality	Accuracy Measure	The reliability and correctness of data	Clean, complete, and consistent data
Data Bias	Imbalance Issue	When data does not represent all groups fairly	Skewed or incomplete datasets
Data Preprocessing	Preparation Step	Cleaning and organizing data before training	Removing errors, formatting text

The Data Family reminds us that artificial intelligence is only as strong as the information it learns from. High-quality data leads to meaningful insights, while poor data can limit or misguide intelligent systems.

Memory Family Introduction

The Memory Family represents how artificial intelligence systems store, retain, and retrieve information. Just as humans rely on memory to recall past experiences, learn new concepts, and make decisions, AI systems depend on memory to access previously processed information and maintain context.

In artificial intelligence, memory is not a single component but a collection of mechanisms that allow systems to handle information over time. Some forms of memory are short-term, holding information temporarily while a task is being completed. Other forms are long-term, storing learned knowledge that can be used across different tasks and interactions.

Memory plays a critical role in enabling AI systems to understand sequences, maintain context in conversations, and improve decision-making. For example, when a user interacts with a language model, the system uses memory to keep track of previous words, sentences, or prompts in order to generate coherent and relevant responses.

The Memory Family works closely with the Data Family, which provides the information to be stored, and the Parameter Family, which encodes learned knowledge within the model. It also supports the Neural Network Family by enabling systems to process sequences and retain important patterns over time.

Understanding the Memory Family helps students see that AI is not simply reacting to individual inputs in isolation. Instead, it relies on stored information and contextual awareness to produce meaningful and consistent outputs.

In simple terms, if data is what AI learns from, memory is how AI remembers and uses what it has learned.

Memory Family Breakdown Chart

Component	Role	Description	Example
Memory	Information Storage	The ability of an AI system to store and access information	Retaining previous inputs in a task
Short-Term Memory	Temporary Storage	Holds information for immediate processing	Keeping track of words in a sentence
Long-Term Memory	Persistent Storage	Stores learned knowledge for future use	Knowledge embedded in model parameters
Context Memory	Conversation Tracking	Maintains information within a specific interaction	Remembering earlier parts of a prompt
Working Memory	Active Processing	Handles information currently being used in computation	Processing a sequence step by step

Component	Role	Description	Example
External Memory	Extended Storage	Memory stored outside the model for retrieval	Databases, vector stores
Internal Memory	Embedded Knowledge	Information stored within the model itself	Learned patterns inside neural networks
Sequence Memory	Order Awareness	Tracks the order of inputs over time	Understanding sentence structure
Retrieval Mechanism	Access System	Retrieves stored information when needed	Searching relevant past data
Attention Mechanism	Focus System	Highlights important parts of memory for processing	Focusing on key words in a sentence
Memory Capacity	Storage Limit	The amount of information the system can handle at once	Context window size

The Memory Family shows that intelligence is not just about processing information in the moment, but about retaining, organizing, and using knowledge over time to create meaningful understanding.

Knowledge Family Introduction

The Knowledge Family represents how artificial intelligence organizes, connects, and uses information to create understanding. While data provides raw information and memory stores it, knowledge is what gives that information meaning and structure.

In artificial intelligence, knowledge is not simply a collection of facts. It is the result of identifying relationships, patterns, and connections within data. AI systems use knowledge to recognize concepts, make decisions, and generate meaningful responses. This allows machines to move beyond simple data processing and toward more intelligent behavior.

Knowledge can be represented in different ways within AI systems. Some forms are structured, such as databases and knowledge graphs, where relationships between concepts are clearly defined. Other forms are learned implicitly through neural networks, where patterns are encoded within parameters and used to guide predictions.

The Knowledge Family works closely with the Data Family, which provides the information needed to build knowledge, and the Memory Family, which stores and retrieves that information. It also connects with the Parameter Family, where learned knowledge is embedded within the model, and the Neural Network Family, which processes and organizes that knowledge.

Understanding the Knowledge Family helps students recognize that AI systems do not simply memorize information. Instead, they learn how pieces of information relate to one another, allowing them to interpret meaning, solve problems, and respond intelligently.

In simple terms, if data is information and memory stores it, knowledge is the understanding that makes it useful.

Knowledge Family Breakdown Chart

Component	Role	Description	Example
Knowledge	Understanding System	Organized information that allows AI to interpret meaning and make decisions	Recognizing relationships between concepts
Facts	Basic Information	Individual pieces of information stored within a system	"Water freezes at 0°C"
Relationships	Connection Mapping	Links between pieces of information that create meaning	"Teacher teaches student"
Knowledge Representation	Structure System	Methods used to organize and store knowledge in AI	Knowledge graphs, semantic networks
Knowledge Graph	Network Mapping	A structured representation of entities and their relationships	Google Knowledge Graph
Semantic Understanding	Meaning Interpretation	The ability to understand meaning behind words and data	Understanding synonyms and context
Inference	Reasoning Process	Drawing conclusions based on known information	If A = B and B = C, then A = C
Rules	Decision Framework	Logical guidelines used to make decisions	If temperature < 0°C → freeze
Ontology	Concept Framework	A structured system defining categories and relationships	Classification of animals
Explicit Knowledge	Direct Information	Clearly defined and stored knowledge	Rules, databases
Implicit Knowledge	Learned Patterns	Knowledge learned through experience and data	Patterns learned by neural networks
Knowledge Integration	System Coordination	Combining information from multiple sources	Merging text, images, and data

The Knowledge Family transforms information into understanding, allowing artificial intelligence to move beyond data and memory into meaningful reasoning and intelligent decision-making.

AI Model Family Introduction

The AI Model Family represents the core system within artificial intelligence that performs tasks such as prediction, classification, and content generation. It is the part of AI that users interact with, whether they are asking questions, generating images, or analyzing data.

An AI model is a trained system that has learned patterns from data. During training, the model processes large amounts of information and adjusts its internal parameters to improve accuracy. Once trained, the model can take new input and produce meaningful output based on what it has learned.

AI models can take many forms depending on their purpose. Some models are designed to recognize images, others to understand language, and others to make decisions or predictions. Large Language Models (LLMs), for example, are designed to process and generate human language by predicting sequences of tokens.

The AI Model Family works closely with the Data Family, which provides the learning material, and the Parameter Family, which stores learned patterns. It also relies on the Neural Network Family for structure and the Chip and Infrastructure Families for execution and deployment.

Understanding the AI Model Family helps students see that AI is not just a concept, but a working system that has been trained to perform specific tasks. It is the engine that transforms input into output.

In simple terms, if AI is the system, the model is the part that actually does the thinking and producing.

AI Model Family Breakdown Chart

Component	Role	Description	Example
AI Model	Core System	The trained system that performs tasks	Chatbot, image generator
Training	Learning Process	Process of teaching the model using data	Learning from datasets
Inference	Output Generation	Using the trained model to produce results	Answering a question
Model Architecture	Structural Design	Defines how the model is built	Neural networks, transformers
Parameters	Learned Values	Internal values adjusted during training	Billions of weights
Input Data	Entry Information	Data provided to the model for processing	User prompt
Output Data	Result	The response or prediction generated	AI-generated text
Model Types	Functional Categories	Different kinds of models for different tasks	Classification, generation
Fine-Tuning	Model Adjustment	Improving a model for specific tasks	Custom-trained AI

Component	Role	Description	Example
Pretrained Model	Base System	A model trained on large datasets before use	General-purpose AI
Evaluation	Performance Check	Measuring how well the model performs	Accuracy, loss metrics

The AI Model Family represents the working core of artificial intelligence, where learned patterns are transformed into meaningful actions, predictions, and responses.

Neural Network Family Introduction

The Neural Network Family represents the structural foundation of how artificial intelligence learns and processes information. Inspired by the human brain, neural networks are systems of interconnected units, often called neurons, that work together to analyze data, recognize patterns, and make decisions.

In artificial intelligence, a neural network is made up of layers. The input layer receives data, the hidden layers process that data, and the output layer produces a result. As information flows through these layers, the network applies mathematical transformations that allow it to detect patterns and relationships within the data.

Neural networks rely heavily on the Parameter Family, where weights and biases determine how strongly information flows between neurons. During training, these parameters are adjusted to improve the network's performance. The more the network learns, the better it becomes at recognizing patterns and making accurate predictions.

The Neural Network Family works closely with the Data Family, which provides the information needed for learning, and the Memory and Knowledge Families, which help store and organize learned information. It also supports the Token Family when processing language, allowing AI systems to interpret sequences of tokens in meaningful ways.

Understanding neural networks helps students see that AI is not simply following instructions. Instead, it is learning from examples and improving over time through layered processing and pattern recognition.

In simple terms, neural networks are the systems that allow AI to think, learn, and make sense of information.

Neural Network Family Breakdown Chart

Component	Role	Description	Example
Neural Network	Learning Structure	A system of interconnected neurons that processes data and learns patterns	Image recognition system
Neuron (Node)	Processing Unit	A basic unit that receives input, processes it, and passes output forward	A single calculation point
Input Layer	Data Entry Point	The first layer that receives raw data	Pixels of an image
Hidden Layers	Processing Layers	Intermediate layers that transform data and detect patterns	Feature detection layers
Output Layer	Result Generator	The final layer that produces predictions or decisions	"Cat" vs "Dog" classification
Weights	Signal Strength	Values that determine how strongly inputs influence outputs	Higher weight = stronger impact
Bias	Adjustment Value	Helps shift outputs to improve learning accuracy	Fine-tuning predictions
Activation Function	Decision Function	Determines whether a neuron should activate based on input	ReLU, Sigmoid
Forward Propagation	Data Flow	The process of passing input data through the network to produce output	Input → Hidden → Output
Backpropagation	Learning Process	Adjusts weights and biases based on error to improve performance	Correcting mistakes
Loss Function	Error Measurement	Calculates how far the output is from the correct answer	Prediction vs actual
Deep Neural Network	Advanced Structure	A network with many hidden layers for complex learning	Deep learning models

The Neural Network Family provides the structure that allows artificial intelligence to transform data into understanding, making it possible for machines to learn from experience and improve over time.

Dual Language System in Artificial Intelligence

Definition

The Dual Language System in Artificial Intelligence refers to the way AI communicates using two different forms of language at the same time: human language for interaction and machine language for internal processing.

Key Components

Human Language (Natural Language)
This is the language people use to communicate with AI, such as English, Spanish, Tongan, or Fijian. It includes words, sentences, and questions that users type or speak.

Machine Language (Numerical Representation)
This is how AI understands information internally. Words are converted into numbers called tokens and processed using mathematical models and algorithms.

How It Works (Step-by-Step)

A user enters a question in human language

The AI converts the words into numerical tokens

The AI processes the tokens using a neural network

The AI generates a response based on patterns and probabilities

The response is converted back into human language

Example

User Input:
"What is Artificial Intelligence?"

AI Process:

Converts words into numbers

Analyzes patterns from training data

Predicts the best possible answer

Output:
"Artificial Intelligence is the ability of machines to perform tasks that normally require human intelligence."

Why This Matters

Understanding the dual language system helps students realize that:

AI does not "think" like humans

AI translates language into math and back into language

Every interaction with AI is based on patterns, not emotions or understanding

Applications

Chatbots and virtual assistants

Language translation systems

Search engines

Voice recognition tools

Challenges

Misinterpretation of human language

Bias in language data

Lack of true understanding or reasoning

Summary

Artificial Intelligence works by translating human language into machine-readable data and then converting the results back into human language. This dual system allows AI to interact with people while operating through mathematical processes behind the scenes.

AI Translator Architecture Family Introduction

The AI Translator Architecture Family represents the system that transforms input into meaningful output in artificial intelligence. It acts as the bridge between what humans provide and what AI produces. Whether a user types a question, uploads an image, or speaks a command, this architecture is responsible for interpreting that input and generating a response.

In artificial intelligence, translation does not only mean converting one language to another. It refers to the broader process of transforming one form of information into another. For example, text can be translated into a response, speech can be converted into text, and images can be interpreted into descriptions. This transformation process is at the core of how modern AI systems function.

The AI Translator Architecture is built on multiple foundational families. It relies on the Token Family to break input into manageable units, the Neural Network Family to process patterns, and the Parameter Family to guide learning. It also uses knowledge and memory to maintain context and produce coherent results.

At the center of this architecture is the ability to encode and decode information. Encoding transforms input into a format the model can understand, while decoding converts processed information back into human-readable output. This continuous transformation allows AI systems to interact with users in a natural and meaningful way.

Understanding the AI Translator Architecture Family helps students see that AI is not simply responding randomly. Instead, it is systematically translating input into output through structured processes and learned patterns.

In simple terms, if tokens are the language pieces and neural networks are the brain, the AI Translator Architecture is the system that turns understanding into communication.

AI Translator Architecture Family Breakdown Chart

Component	Role	Description	Example
AI Translator Architecture	Transformation System	Converts input into meaningful output	Question → Answer
Input Processing	Data Intake	Receives and prepares user input for analysis	Text prompt entered by a user
Encoding	Input Conversion	Transforms input into numerical representations	Words → token IDs
Context Building	Meaning Formation	Organizes input into a structured understanding	Sentence context tracking
Sequence Processing	Order Handling	Maintains the correct order of information	Word sequence in a sentence
Attention Mechanism	Focus System	Identifies important parts of input data	Highlighting key words
Representation Layer	Feature Mapping	Converts data into internal representations for processing	Embeddings
Decoding	Output Generation	Converts processed data back into human-readable form	Token IDs → words
Output Generation	Response Creation	Produces the final answer or result	AI-generated response
Multimodal Translation	Cross-Format Processing	Translates between different types of data	Image → text description
Feedback Loop	Improvement Cycle	Uses results to refine future outputs	Model learning over time

The AI Translator Architecture Family shows that artificial intelligence is not just about understanding information, but about transforming it into meaningful communication that humans can use and interact with.

AI Architecture Family Introduction

The AI Architecture Family represents the overall design and structure of an artificial intelligence system. While individual families such as Data, Parameters, and Neural Networks explain how AI learns and processes information, the AI Architecture Family shows how all these components are organized and work together as a complete system.

In artificial intelligence, architecture refers to the blueprint that defines how data flows through a system, how components interact, and how decisions are produced. It determines how input is received, how it is processed, and how output is generated. A well-designed architecture allows AI systems to operate efficiently, scale to large problems, and produce reliable results.

AI architectures can vary depending on the type of system being built. Some are designed for image recognition, others for language processing, and others for decision-making or automation. Despite these differences, most architectures share common elements such as input layers, processing layers, memory components, and output mechanisms.

The AI Architecture Family connects all foundational families. It integrates the Data Family for input, the Token Family for language processing, the Neural Network Family for computation, the Parameter Family for learning, and the Memory and Knowledge Families for storing and organizing information. It also works closely with the AI Translator Architecture Family to transform input into meaningful output.

Understanding the AI Architecture Family helps students see the “big picture” of artificial intelligence. Instead of viewing AI as separate parts, they begin to understand it as a coordinated system where each component plays a specific role.

In simple terms, if individual families are the parts of AI, the AI Architecture Family is the blueprint that brings everything together into one working system.

AI Architecture Family Breakdown Chart

Component	Role	Description	Example
AI Architecture	System Blueprint	The overall design that defines how an AI system is structured and operates	ChatGPT system design

Component	Role	Description	Example
Input Layer	Data Entry Point	Receives raw input from users or external sources	Text prompt, image upload
Preprocessing Layer	Data Preparation	Cleans and organizes input data before processing	Tokenization, normalization
Processing Core	Computation Engine	The main system where data is analyzed and transformed	Neural networks, transformers
Parameter System	Learning Core	Stores adjustable values that guide learning and predictions	Model weights and biases
Memory System	Context Storage	Maintains and retrieves information during processing	Context window, external memory
Knowledge System	Understanding Layer	Organizes relationships and meaning within the system	Knowledge graphs, learned patterns
Decision Layer	Output Logic	Determines the final output based on processed data	Selecting the best response
Output Layer	Result Delivery	Presents results to the user in a usable format	Text, image, or audio response
Feedback Loop	Improvement System	Uses outcomes to refine future performance	Model updates and retraining
Scalability System	Expansion Capability	Allows the system to handle increasing data and complexity	Cloud-based AI systems
Integration Layer	System Connection	Connects AI with external tools and platforms	APIs, databases, applications

The AI Architecture Family reveals that artificial intelligence is not a single technology, but a coordinated system of interconnected components working together to transform data into intelligent outcomes.

Chip Family Introduction

The Chip Family represents the physical hardware that powers artificial intelligence systems. While software components such as data, algorithms, and neural networks define how AI works, none of these systems can function without the computing chips that perform the actual calculations.

Chips are specialized electronic components designed to process information at extremely high speeds. In artificial intelligence, these chips handle the complex mathematical operations required for training models and generating outputs. Every prediction, calculation, and response produced by an AI system is executed by hardware within the Chip Family.

Different types of chips are used depending on the needs of the system. Central Processing Units (CPUs) handle general-purpose tasks, while Graphics Processing Units (GPUs) are optimized for parallel processing, making them ideal for training neural networks. More specialized chips, such as Tensor Processing Units (TPUs) and Neural Processing Units (NPUs), are designed specifically for AI workloads, enabling faster and more efficient computation.

The Chip Family works closely with the Neural Network Family, which defines the structure of computation, and the Parameter Family, which stores the values being processed. It also connects to the Infrastructure Family, where large-scale systems of chips are organized in data centers and cloud environments.

Understanding the Chip Family helps students recognize that artificial intelligence is not purely abstract. It depends on physical machines that require power, resources, and engineering to operate. These chips are the engines that bring AI models to life.

In simple terms, if AI is the intelligence, chips are the machines that make that intelligence possible.

Chip Family Breakdown Chart

Component	Role	Description	Example
Chip (Processor)	Computation Engine	Electronic hardware that performs calculations required for AI	CPU, GPU
CPU (Central Processing Unit)	General Processor	Handles a wide range of computing tasks	Running basic applications
GPU (Graphics Processing Unit)	Parallel Processor	Processes many calculations at once, ideal for AI training	Training neural networks
TPU (Tensor Processing Unit)	AI Accelerator	Specialized chip designed for machine learning tasks	Google TPU
NPU (Neural Processing Unit)	Edge AI Processor	Optimized for running AI on devices like phones	Smartphone AI features
AI Accelerator	Performance Booster	Hardware designed to speed up AI computations	Dedicated AI chips
Memory (Hardware)	Data Storage	Stores data and instructions for processing	RAM, VRAM
Parallel Processing	Speed Mechanism	Ability to perform multiple calculations simultaneously	GPUs processing thousands of operations
Throughput	Processing Capacity	Amount of data processed over time	High-performance computing systems
Latency	Response Time	Time it takes to process a request	Faster chips = lower latency
Power Consumption	Energy Usage	Amount of energy required to run the chip	High-performance GPUs use more power

Component	Role	Description	Example
Edge Devices	Local Processing	Devices that run AI locally without cloud support	Phones, smart cameras

The Chip Family reminds us that behind every intelligent system is powerful hardware performing millions or billions of calculations, turning abstract models into real-world functionality.

Watts Family Introduction

The Watts Family represents the measurement of power used by artificial intelligence systems. While the Chip Family provides the hardware that performs computations, the Watts Family explains how much energy those systems consume while operating.

A watt is a unit of power that measures the rate at which energy is used. In artificial intelligence, watts help us understand how much electricity is required to run processors, train models, and generate responses. Every time an AI system processes data, performs calculations, or produces output, it consumes power.

Different AI systems require different levels of power depending on their size and complexity. Small systems, such as those running on mobile devices, use relatively low amounts of power. In contrast, large-scale AI models operating in data centers can require significant amounts of electricity, especially during training, where billions of calculations are performed continuously.

The Watts Family works closely with the Chip Family, which determines how efficiently computations are performed, and the Infrastructure Family, where large networks of machines operate together. It also connects to the overall design of AI systems, as more efficient models can reduce power consumption while maintaining performance.

Understanding the Watts Family helps students recognize that artificial intelligence is not only about intelligence and computation, but also about energy use and resource management. As AI continues to grow, managing power efficiently becomes an important part of building responsible and sustainable systems.

In simple terms, if chips perform the work, watts measure how much power it takes to do that work.

Watts Family Breakdown Chart

Component	Role	Description	Example
Watt (W)	Power Measurement	Unit that measures the rate of energy use	A device using 100 watts
Power Consumption	Energy Usage Rate	Amount of power used during operation	AI model running on GPUs
Energy Efficiency	Performance Balance	How effectively a system uses power to perform tasks	More output with less power
High-Performance Computing	Intensive Power Use	Systems that require large amounts of power for complex tasks	AI training clusters
Idle Power	Standby Usage	Power consumed when systems are not actively processing	Servers waiting for requests
Peak Power	Maximum Usage	Highest level of power used during heavy workloads	Training large AI models
Thermal Output	Heat Generation	Heat produced as a result of power usage	Cooling systems in data centers
Cooling Systems	Temperature Control	Systems used to manage heat from high power usage	Air or liquid cooling
Power Supply	Energy Source	Provides electricity to AI systems	Electrical grid, batteries
Edge Power Usage	Local Energy Use	Power consumption on smaller devices	Smartphones, IoT devices
Data Center Power	Large-Scale Usage	Power required for large AI operations	Server farms running AI models
Sustainable Energy	Efficiency Goal	Use of renewable energy to reduce environmental impact	Solar-powered data centers

The Watts Family highlights that intelligence comes with a cost—every AI system requires power, and understanding that power is essential for building efficient and sustainable technologies.

Watts Family (AI Power Usage Scale)

Definition

The **Watts Family** represents the real-time power usage of artificial intelligence systems, measured in watts (W). It shows how much power AI systems consume at a given moment as they process data and perform computations.

Watts Scale

1 Watt
10 Watts

100 Watts
500 Watts
1,000 Watts (1 Kilowatt)
10,000 Watts (10 Kilowatts)
100,000 Watts (100 Kilowatts)
1,000,000 Watts (1 Megawatt)
10,000,000 Watts (10 Megawatts)
100,000,000+ Watts (100+ Megawatts)

Key Characteristics

Measured in real-world electrical power

Higher watt values indicate higher processing demand

Used to represent the scale of AI systems from small devices to large infrastructures

Closely connected to the Chip Family, Energy Family, and Infrastructure Family

Examples

Low watts → small devices and basic AI functions

Medium watts → computers and advanced applications

High watts → data centers and large AI systems

Summary

The **Watts Family** provides a numerical representation of how much power artificial intelligence systems use in real time, helping to illustrate the scale and intensity of AI operations.

Student Insight

Watts show how much power AI is using right now.

AI Energy Family Introduction

The AI Energy Family represents the total amount of energy consumed by artificial intelligence systems over time. While the Watts Family measures the rate at which power is used at any given moment, the Energy Family focuses on the accumulated energy required to perform tasks, run systems, and sustain operations.

In artificial intelligence, energy is used every time a model is trained, a system processes data, or a response is generated. Large-scale AI systems, especially those operating in data centers, can consume significant amounts of energy due to the continuous processing of massive datasets and complex computations.

Energy is typically measured over time using units such as kilowatt-hours (kWh), which reflect how much power has been used during a specific period. For example, running a high-performance AI system for several hours or days results in a total energy cost that goes beyond the moment-to-moment power usage measured in watts.

The AI Energy Family works closely with the Watts Family, which provides the rate of power consumption, and the Chip Family, which determines how efficiently computations are performed. It also connects to the Infrastructure Family, where large-scale systems operate continuously and require long-term energy management.

Understanding the AI Energy Family helps students recognize that artificial intelligence has real-world resource implications. It is not only about performance and speed, but also about sustainability, efficiency, and responsible use of technology.

In simple terms, if watts measure how fast energy is used, energy measures how much is used over time.

AI Energy Family Breakdown Chart

Component	Role	Description	Example
Energy	Total Consumption	The total amount of power used over a period of time	Running an AI system for hours or days
Kilowatt-hour (kWh)	Energy Measurement	Unit used to measure energy consumption over time	1 kWh = using 1,000 watts for 1 hour
Energy Usage	Consumption Tracking	Total energy required for AI operations	Training a large model
Training Energy	Learning Cost	Energy used during model training processes	Weeks of GPU usage
Inference Energy	Response Cost	Energy used when AI generates outputs	Answering a user prompt
Energy Efficiency	Optimization Goal	Reducing energy use while maintaining performance	Efficient AI models
Energy Scaling	Growth Impact	Increase in energy use as systems grow larger	Bigger models = more energy
Data Center Energy	Infrastructure Demand	Total energy used by large AI facilities	Server farms operating 24/7

Component	Role	Description	Example
Cooling Energy	Temperature Control	Energy required to cool systems and prevent overheating	Air conditioning in data centers
Renewable Energy	Sustainability Source	Use of clean energy to power AI systems	Solar, wind-powered data centers
Carbon Impact	Environmental Effect	Emissions associated with energy consumption	AI training carbon footprint
Energy Management	Resource Control	Strategies to monitor and reduce energy use	Efficient scheduling, hardware optimization

The AI Energy Family reminds us that artificial intelligence operates within the physical world, where every computation consumes energy and every system has an impact on resources and sustainability.

Energy Family (Total Power Consumption of Artificial Intelligence)

Definition

The **Energy Family** represents the total amount of electricity used by artificial intelligence systems over time. It is measured in watt-hours (Wh) or kilowatt-hours (kWh) and shows how much energy AI systems consume while running.

Energy Scale

1 Watt-hour (Wh)
10 Watt-hours (Wh)
100 Watt-hours (Wh)
500 Watt-hours (Wh)
1,000 Watt-hours (1 Kilowatt-hour, kWh)
10,000 Watt-hours (10 kWh)
100,000 Watt-hours (100 kWh)
1,000,000 Watt-hours (1 Megawatt-hour, MWh)
10,000,000 Watt-hours (10 MWh)
100,000,000+ Watt-hours (100+ MWh)

Key Characteristics

Measured over time (not instant like watts)

Represents total electricity consumption

Increases the longer AI systems run

Directly related to cost and energy usage

Closely connected to Watts Family, Chip Family, and Infrastructure Family

Examples

Low energy → short AI tasks or small devices

Medium energy → daily AI usage on computers

High energy → training AI models and running data centers

Summary

The **Energy Family** provides a numerical representation of the total electricity consumed by artificial intelligence systems over time, helping to illustrate the overall cost and impact of AI operations.

Student Insight

Energy shows how much total power AI has used over time.

AI Infrastructure Family Introduction

The AI Infrastructure Family represents the large-scale systems and environments that support, power, and connect artificial intelligence technologies. While individual components such as chips, data, and models explain how AI works, infrastructure explains where and how these systems operate in the real world.

AI infrastructure includes data centers, cloud platforms, networking systems, and storage environments that allow artificial intelligence to function at scale. These systems provide the computing power, data access, and connectivity needed to train models, process information, and deliver results to users around the world.

Modern AI systems rely heavily on cloud-based infrastructure, where thousands of machines work together to handle massive workloads. This allows AI to scale efficiently, making it possible to process large datasets, run complex models, and serve millions of users simultaneously. Infrastructure also ensures reliability, security, and continuous availability of AI services.

The AI Infrastructure Family works closely with the Chip Family, which provides the hardware, the Watts and Energy Families, which manage power consumption, and the Data Family, which supplies the information being processed. It also supports the AI Architecture Family by providing the environment where all system components are deployed and connected.

Understanding the AI Infrastructure Family helps students recognize that artificial intelligence is not contained within a single device. Instead, it operates across global systems that require coordination, resources, and engineering to function effectively.

In simple terms, if AI is the system and chips are the engines, infrastructure is the environment that allows everything to run at scale.

AI Infrastructure Family Breakdown Chart

Component	Role	Description	Example
AI Infrastructure	System Environment	The physical and digital systems that support AI operations	Global AI platforms
Data Center	Processing Hub	Facilities that house servers and computing equipment	Large server farms
Cloud Computing	Scalable Platform	Remote systems that provide computing resources over the internet	AWS, Azure, Google Cloud
Servers	Compute Units	Machines that process data and run AI models	Rack-mounted servers
Networking	Connectivity System	Systems that allow communication between machines	Internet, fiber networks
Storage Systems	Data Management	Systems that store large volumes of data	Databases, cloud storage
Distributed Computing	Workload Sharing	Splitting tasks across multiple machines for efficiency	Parallel processing across clusters
Edge Infrastructure	Local Processing	Running AI closer to the user or device	Smart devices, IoT systems
Load Balancing	Traffic Control	Distributes workloads to prevent overload	Managing user requests
Security Systems	Protection Layer	Safeguards data and systems from threats	Encryption, firewalls
Redundancy	Reliability System	Backup systems to ensure continuous operation	Failover servers
Scalability	Growth Capability	Ability to expand resources as demand increases	Adding more servers dynamically

The AI Infrastructure Family reveals that artificial intelligence operates on a global scale, relying on interconnected systems that provide the power, storage, and connectivity needed to support intelligent technologies.

AI Agent Family Introduction

The AI Agent Family represents systems that can take action, make decisions, and perform tasks on behalf of users or other systems. Unlike traditional AI models that only respond to input, AI agents are designed to operate with a level of autonomy, allowing them to plan, execute, and adapt to achieve specific goals.

An AI agent receives input from its environment, processes that information, and takes actions based on predefined objectives or learned behaviors. These actions can include answering questions, automating workflows, retrieving information, or interacting with other systems. Some agents operate in simple environments, while others function in complex systems that require continuous decision-making.

AI agents often combine multiple foundational families. They use the Data Family to gather information, the Memory and Knowledge Families to retain and understand context, and the Neural Network and Parameter Families to process and learn from interactions. They also rely on the AI Architecture and Infrastructure Families to operate reliably at scale.

Modern AI agents can work independently or as part of larger systems. For example, a customer support agent can respond to inquiries automatically, while a more advanced agent can complete multi-step tasks such as scheduling, research, or system management.

Understanding the AI Agent Family helps students see that artificial intelligence is not only about generating responses, but also about taking meaningful action in real-world scenarios.

In simple terms, if AI models think and respond, AI agents act and execute.

AI Agent Family Breakdown Chart

Component	Role	Description	Example
AI Agent	Action System	An AI system that can make decisions and perform tasks	Virtual assistant
Environment	Operating Context	The space where the agent interacts and gathers information	Web, apps, databases
Input Perception	Data Intake	Receives information from the environment	User query or sensor input

Component	Role	Description	Example
Decision Engine	Action Selection	Determines what action to take based on input	Choosing a response or task
Action Execution	Task Performance	Carries out decisions in the environment	Sending an email, retrieving data
Goal System	Objective Setting	Defines what the agent is trying to achieve	Complete a task or solve a problem
Planning Module	Strategy Builder	Breaks down tasks into steps	Multi-step problem solving
Feedback Loop	Learning Cycle	Improves performance based on outcomes	Adjusting actions over time
Autonomy Level	Independence Scale	Degree of independence in decision-making	Fully automated vs assisted
Multi-Agent System	Collaboration Network	Multiple agents working together	Coordinated AI systems

Ingredient Family Introduction

The Ingredient Family represents the essential components that come together to create an artificial intelligence system. Just as a recipe requires specific ingredients to produce a final dish, AI systems rely on a combination of foundational elements working together to function effectively.

Artificial intelligence is not built from a single component. It requires data to learn from, algorithms to guide processing, models to perform tasks, hardware to execute computations, and energy to power the entire system. Each of these elements plays a critical role, and the absence of any one component would prevent the system from operating properly.

The Ingredient Family provides a simplified way for students to understand AI as a system made up of interconnected parts. Instead of viewing AI as complex or mysterious, learners can begin to see it as something constructed from identifiable and understandable components.

This family connects directly with all other foundational families, including Data, Algorithm, Neural Network, Parameter, Chip, and Energy Families. It serves as an overview that brings these elements together into a unified perspective.

Understanding the Ingredient Family helps students recognize that artificial intelligence is built, not magical. It is the result of carefully combining the right components in the right way.

In simple terms, if AI is the final product, the Ingredient Family represents everything needed to build it.

Ingredient Family Breakdown Chart

Component	Role	Description	Example
Data	Learning Input	Provides the information AI uses to learn patterns	Text, images, audio
Algorithms	Instruction Set	Guides how data is processed and decisions are made	Sorting, classification
AI Models	Execution System	Performs tasks such as prediction or generation	Language models
Neural Networks	Processing Structure	Organizes how data is processed through layers	Deep learning models
Parameters	Learning Adjustments	Fine-tune how the model learns and makes predictions	Weights and biases
Tokens	Language Units	Breaks text into smaller pieces for processing	Words or subwords
Hardware (Chips)	Computation Engine	Executes calculations required by AI systems	GPUs, CPUs
Energy	Power Source	Supplies the energy needed to run systems	Electricity usage
Infrastructure	Support System	Provides the environment for AI to operate at scale	Cloud systems, data centers
Memory	Storage System	Stores and retrieves information for processing	Context memory
Knowledge	Understanding Layer	Represents meaning and relationships within data	Knowledge graphs

The Ingredient Family shows that artificial intelligence is built from a combination of essential components, each playing a vital role in creating intelligent systems.

The Frontend and Backend Family of Artificial Intelligence

How AI Systems Connect User Interaction to Intelligent Processing

Introduction

Every artificial intelligence system operates through two essential layers: the frontend and the backend. These layers work together to transform human interaction into intelligent responses, allowing AI systems to function smoothly and effectively.

The frontend is the part of the system that users see and interact with. It includes screens, input tools, and the display of results. Whether a user is typing a question, speaking a command, or uploading an image, all interaction begins at the frontend.

Behind the scenes, the backend serves as the processing engine of the system. It receives input from the frontend, manages data, connects to the AI model, and performs the computations needed to generate a response. The backend is where the intelligence of the system operates, using models, algorithms, and infrastructure to interpret and respond to user requests.

This visual illustrates how these two layers work together as a complete system. It shows the flow of information from user input to AI processing and back to the user as a result. By understanding this structure, students can see that AI is not a single tool, but a coordinated system of layers working together.

In simple terms, the frontend is where interaction happens, and the backend is where intelligence is created.

Every AI system has two sides: what you see and what actually does the thinking.

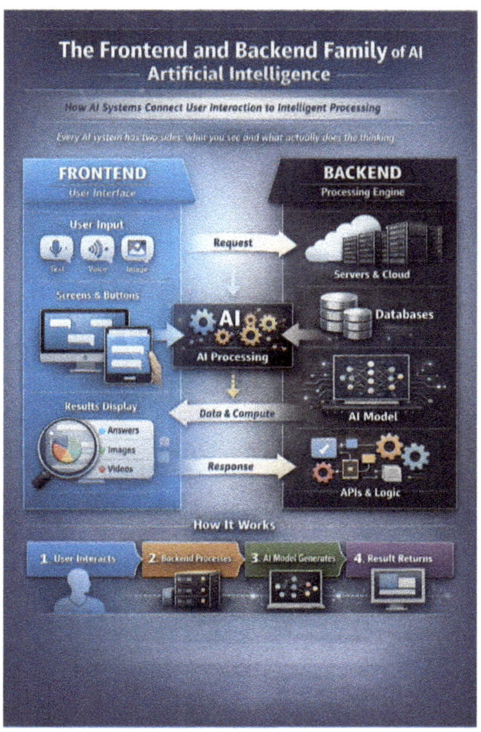

AI Qubit Family Introduction

The AI Qubit Family represents the foundation of quantum computing as it relates to artificial intelligence. While traditional computing relies on bits, which can exist as either 0 or 1, quantum computing uses qubits, which can exist in multiple states simultaneously.

A qubit is the basic unit of quantum information. Unlike classical bits, qubits can take advantage of properties such as superposition and entanglement, allowing quantum systems to process complex computations more efficiently in certain scenarios. This opens new possibilities for solving problems that are difficult or impossible for traditional computers.

In the context of artificial intelligence, qubits have the potential to accelerate learning processes, optimize large-scale systems, and improve complex simulations. Although quantum AI is still in development, it represents a future direction where computational power can expand beyond current limitations.

The AI Qubit Family connects with the Chip Family, as quantum processors are specialized hardware, and with the Algorithm Family, where new types of quantum algorithms are designed. It also relates to the Parameter and Neural Network Families, as researchers explore quantum-enhanced learning models.

Understanding the AI Qubit Family helps students see that artificial intelligence is continuously evolving. It introduces the idea that the foundations of computing themselves can change, leading to new forms of intelligence and problem-solving.

In simple terms, if bits are the foundation of today's computing, qubits represent the foundation of tomorrow's possibilities.

AI Qubit Family Breakdown Chart

Component	Role	Description	Example
Qubit	Quantum Unit	Basic unit of quantum information	Quantum bit in a quantum computer
Superposition	Multi-State Ability	Ability to exist in multiple states at once	0 and 1 simultaneously
Entanglement	Connection Property	Linking qubits so they influence each other	Paired quantum states
Quantum Gate	Operation System	Performs operations on qubits	Quantum logic gates
Quantum Circuit	Processing Structure	Sequence of quantum operations	Quantum algorithms
Quantum Processor	Hardware Engine	Specialized chip for quantum computing	Quantum computer hardware
Quantum Algorithm	Computation Method	Algorithm designed for quantum systems	Optimization problems
Quantum Speedup	Performance Advantage	Faster processing for certain problems	Complex simulations
Quantum Noise	Stability Challenge	Errors caused by environmental interference	Qubit instability
Quantum Error Correction	Stability Solution	Techniques to reduce errors in quantum systems	Fault-tolerant computing

The AI Qubit Family introduces a new frontier in computing, where the limits of traditional systems are expanded, opening the door to more powerful and advanced forms of artificial intelligence.

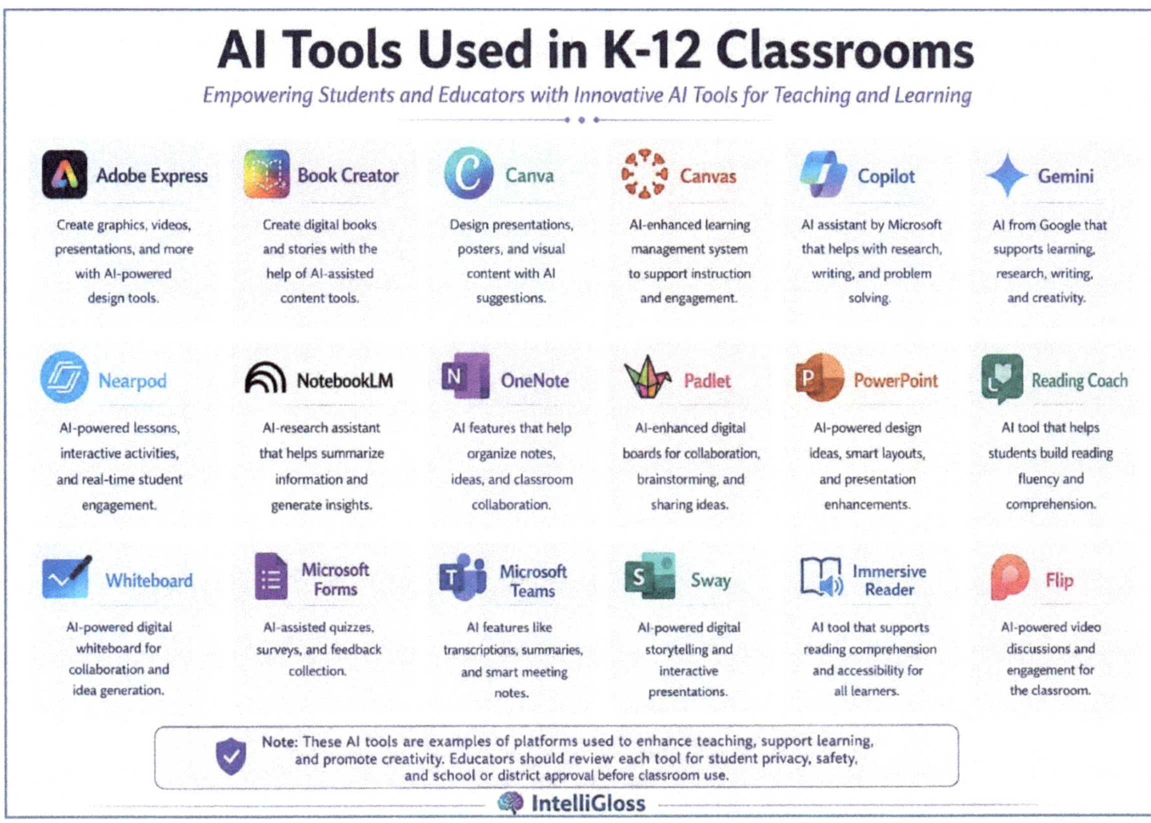

TABLE OF CONTENTS

Introduction

Artificial intelligence is often described as a machine that can learn, reason, recognize patterns, and make decisions. These abilities can seem almost magical, leading many people to believe that AI simply "knows" things. In reality, artificial intelligence does not possess human senses or awareness. It cannot see a traffic light, hear a conversation, feel the temperature of a room, or detect the movement of a person unless specialized technologies collect that information first. Every intelligent decision made by an AI system begins with one essential ingredient: data gathered from sensors.

At this very moment, while you are reading this book, billions of sensors are quietly working around the world. Satellites orbit high above Earth, capturing images of cities, forests, oceans, and weather systems. Cameras monitor roads, businesses, schools, and public spaces. Smartphones determine their location using satellites while measuring movement through tiny accelerometers and gyroscopes. Smart watches monitor heart rates and physical activity. Self-driving vehicles constantly scan their surroundings using cameras, radar, and lidar. Factories use sensors to detect equipment failures before they occur. Hospitals rely on medical sensors to monitor patients and assist doctors in making critical decisions. Together, these technologies create a vast network that allows artificial intelligence to observe and interact with the world.

This global network is known as the **AI Sensor Ecosystem**. It consists of billions of connected devices that continuously collect information about the physical environment. These sensors act as the eyes, ears, touch, balance, and awareness systems of artificial intelligence. Without them, AI would have no information to analyze, no patterns to recognize, and no basis for making decisions. Sensors transform the physical world into digital information that computers can process, making intelligent automation possible across nearly every industry.

Many people think of AI as software running inside a computer. While software is an important part of artificial intelligence, AI is much more than computer code. Modern AI depends on an enormous infrastructure of hardware that constantly gathers information from the real world. Cameras provide images, microphones capture sound, GPS receivers determine location, environmental sensors measure temperature and air quality, satellites observe changes across continents, and industrial machines monitor manufacturing processes every second of the day. These technologies work together to create a continuous stream of information that AI systems use to understand what is happening around them.

As artificial intelligence continues to expand, the number of connected devices is growing rapidly. Experts estimate that tens of billions of Internet-connected devices are already operating worldwide, with many more expected to be added over the coming years. Every new sensor contributes additional information that can improve AI systems, making them more accurate, responsive, and capable of solving increasingly complex problems. From agriculture and healthcare to transportation, education, manufacturing, and environmental protection, sensors have become the foundation that allows AI to improve efficiency, safety, and decision-making.

However, the growth of the AI Sensor Ecosystem also introduces important questions. How much information should be collected? Who owns the data generated by billions of connected devices? How can privacy be protected while still allowing AI to improve our lives? How do governments, businesses, schools, and individuals balance innovation with responsible technology use? These questions have become some of the most significant ethical challenges of the digital age and require thoughtful discussion alongside technological progress.

Throughout this book, you will discover how sensors give artificial intelligence the ability to perceive its environment, how different types of sensors work together, and how they power many of the AI applications used every day. You will explore the technologies behind autonomous vehicles, smart cities, satellites, robotics, healthcare systems, industrial automation, and the Internet of Things. Along the way, you will also examine the responsibilities that come with building a world where intelligent machines are increasingly connected to every aspect of society.

By the time you finish this book, you will understand that artificial intelligence is not simply about algorithms or computer programs. It is about creating intelligent systems that can collect information, interpret their surroundings, make informed decisions, and assist people in solving real-world problems. Understanding the AI Sensor Ecosystem provides one of the final pieces needed to understand today's artificial intelligence before exploring the more advanced intelligent systems that await in the next stage of your AI learning journey.

Welcome to **The AI Sensor Ecosystem**—where artificial intelligence begins to perceive, understand, and connect with the world around us.

Learn AI. Understand AI. Shape the Future.

— Susie Hala
IntelliGloss Press

Chapter 1

The AI Sensor Ecosystem: Giving Artificial Intelligence the Ability to Perceive the World

Artificial intelligence is often described as a technology that can learn, reason, recognize patterns, solve problems, and make decisions. These descriptions are accurate, but they leave out one of the most important pieces of the puzzle. Before an AI system can learn anything, it must first collect information about the world around it. Just as people depend on their eyes to see, ears to hear, skin to feel, and other senses to understand their surroundings, artificial intelligence also requires a way to gather information. Unlike humans, however, AI does not possess biological senses. Instead, it depends on an enormous network of electronic devices known as **sensors**. These sensors serve as the connection between the physical world and the digital world, allowing AI to observe, measure, and understand what is happening in its environment.

Imagine waking up in the morning and suddenly losing every one of your senses. You could no longer see the sunrise through your window, hear your alarm clock, smell breakfast cooking, feel the warmth of sunlight, or tell whether you were standing or sitting. Your brain would still exist, but without information from your senses, it would have almost nothing to think about. This simple example illustrates why sensors are so important for artificial intelligence. AI may contain advanced algorithms, powerful processors, and sophisticated mathematical models, but without a continuous flow of information, it cannot recognize patterns, make predictions, or perform useful work. Data is the fuel that powers artificial intelligence, and sensors are the tools that collect that fuel.

The relationship between sensors and AI can be compared to the relationship between the human nervous system and the brain. The brain depends on billions of nerve cells that carry information from different parts of the body. When you touch a hot stove, sensory nerves immediately send electrical signals to your brain, which quickly tells your muscles to pull your hand away. Artificial intelligence follows a similar pattern. A camera captures an image, a microphone records sound, a temperature sensor measures heat, or a GPS receiver determines location. These electronic signals are converted into digital data that AI systems analyze to determine what is happening and decide what action to take. Although the technology is different, the principle is remarkably similar: no intelligence can operate effectively without information.

Every day, people interact with AI sensor systems without even realizing it. When you unlock your smartphone using facial recognition, the front camera captures your face and AI compares it with a secure digital template stored on your device. When your navigation app calculates the fastest route home, GPS satellites determine your location while traffic sensors provide real-time information about road conditions. When a smartwatch monitors your heart rate during exercise, tiny optical sensors measure changes in blood flow beneath your skin. Voice assistants listen for spoken commands through microphones, while security cameras use computer vision to detect movement or identify objects. Even the automatic doors at grocery stores rely on motion sensors to detect approaching customers. Each of these examples demonstrates how sensors quietly gather information that AI systems transform into useful actions.

As technology continues to advance, these individual devices are becoming part of something much larger. Instead of operating independently, billions of connected sensors now communicate across networks that span homes, businesses, cities, factories, farms, hospitals, transportation systems, and even outer space. This worldwide network is called the **AI Sensor Ecosystem**. It represents one of the largest technological infrastructures ever created by humanity. Satellites orbiting hundreds of miles above Earth continuously capture images of forests, oceans, cities, and weather systems. Drones inspect power lines, monitor crops, and assist emergency responders after natural disasters. Autonomous vehicles use cameras, radar, and lidar to understand traffic conditions and avoid obstacles. Industrial machines constantly monitor pressure, vibration, temperature, and energy consumption to detect problems before equipment fails. Together, these technologies create a continuous stream of information that allows AI systems to understand events occurring across the globe.

One of the most remarkable characteristics of the AI Sensor Ecosystem is that it never sleeps. Unlike humans, who require rest, sensor networks operate twenty-four hours a day, seven days a week. Weather satellites continue tracking hurricanes throughout the night. Environmental sensors monitor air quality and water conditions every minute of the day. Smart electrical grids measure energy demand and automatically balance power distribution across entire cities. Manufacturing facilities collect millions of measurements every hour to improve product quality and reduce waste. Hospitals continuously monitor patients' heart rates, oxygen levels, and other vital signs to alert medical staff if a condition changes. Every second, enormous quantities of new information are added to the growing digital picture of our world.

However, collecting information is only the first step. Raw sensor data has little value until artificial intelligence transforms it into meaningful knowledge. Consider a digital camera attached to a self-driving car. The camera captures millions of tiny colored pixels, but the camera itself does not know whether it is looking at a stop sign, a child crossing the street, or another vehicle. AI algorithms analyze those pixels, compare them with patterns learned from millions of previous images, and identify what each object represents. This process happens many times every second, allowing the vehicle to safely respond to changing road conditions. Similar processes occur in medical imaging, satellite observation, robotics, manufacturing, agriculture, and countless other industries where AI converts raw measurements into useful information.

As the AI Sensor Ecosystem grows larger, it also creates new responsibilities. Every sensor collects data, and every piece of data raises important questions about privacy, security, ownership, and ethics. Who should have access to information collected by smart devices? How can organizations protect sensitive personal data from cyberattacks? How do governments encourage innovation while respecting individual rights? Can AI systems remain fair if the data collected by sensors contains errors or hidden biases? These questions remind us that technology alone is never enough. Responsible AI requires responsible people who understand not only how these systems work but also how they should be used to benefit society.

Understanding the AI Sensor Ecosystem helps us see artificial intelligence from a much broader perspective. AI is not simply software running inside a computer. It is part of a vast interconnected system that links the physical and digital worlds together. Cameras become AI's eyes. Microphones become its ears. GPS becomes its sense of location. Lidar, radar, and infrared sensors allow AI to detect objects that humans cannot easily perceive. Satellites provide a global view of our planet, while billions of connected devices continuously contribute information that expands AI's understanding of the environment. Together, these technologies create intelligent systems capable of helping people solve problems that were once considered impossible.

As you continue reading this book, you will discover that sensors are far more than electronic components hidden inside machines. They are the foundation upon which modern artificial intelligence is built. Every intelligent recommendation, every autonomous decision, every smart device, and every advanced robotic system begins with information collected from the world around it. By understanding how sensors gather data and how AI transforms that data into knowledge, you will gain a deeper appreciation of the invisible technological ecosystem that is quietly shaping the future of humanity. The more you understand how AI perceives the world, the better prepared you will be to participate in a future where intelligent systems become an even greater part of everyday life.

Learn AI. Understand AI. Shape the Future.

— Susie Hala
IntelliGloss Press

Chapter 1 Summary

Chapter 1 introduced the concept of the **AI Sensor Ecosystem**, the worldwide network of sensors that allows artificial intelligence to gather information about the physical world. Unlike humans, AI does not naturally see, hear, touch, or sense its surroundings. Instead, it depends on electronic sensors such as cameras, microphones, GPS receivers, lidar, radar, and many other devices to collect data.

The chapter explained that sensors are the foundation of modern AI because they provide the information that AI systems need to recognize patterns, make decisions, and perform useful tasks. Readers learned that AI is much more than software running on computers. It is connected to billions of devices that continuously gather information from homes, schools, businesses, hospitals, factories, vehicles, satellites, and smart cities.

The chapter also explored how AI transforms raw sensor data into meaningful knowledge. Cameras collect images, microphones capture sound, GPS devices determine location, and environmental sensors measure conditions such as temperature and air quality. AI analyzes these different types of information to understand what is happening and determine the best response.

Finally, the chapter emphasized that as AI becomes more connected to everyday life, society must carefully consider important issues such as privacy, cybersecurity, ethics, and responsible data use. Understanding the AI Sensor Ecosystem helps readers appreciate how AI interacts with the world and prepares them to study more advanced AI technologies throughout the remainder of this book.

Reflection

Artificial intelligence often appears to be intelligent because we focus on what it can do rather than how it gathers information. This chapter reminds us that AI depends entirely on data collected through sensors. Every recommendation, prediction, or automated decision begins with information gathered from the physical world.

As AI continues to expand into healthcare, education, transportation, agriculture, manufacturing, and everyday life, understanding where AI gets its information becomes just as important as understanding how AI processes that information. Future innovators, educators, and decision-makers must recognize that technology should improve people's lives while respecting privacy, security, and ethical responsibilities.

The AI Sensor Ecosystem demonstrates that intelligence is not created by algorithms alone. It is created through the partnership of sensors, data, computing power, and responsible human design.

Student Worksheet

Name: ______________________________

Part A – Vocabulary

Define each term using your own words.

1. AI Sensor Ecosystem

____

2. Sensor

____

3. Data

____

4. Computer Vision

____

5. Internet of Things (IoT)

____

____

Part B – Short Answer

1. Why can't artificial intelligence function without sensors?

2. Name four different types of sensors discussed in this chapter.

3. How is the AI Sensor Ecosystem similar to the human nervous system?

4. Give two examples of AI systems that use sensors every day.

5. Why are privacy and ethics important in the AI Sensor Ecosystem?

Part C – Critical Thinking

Imagine your school wants to become a "smart school" using AI.

Write one paragraph explaining:

- What sensors might be installed?
- How could AI improve learning?
- What privacy concerns should be considered?

Chapter 1 Quiz

Multiple Choice

1. What allows artificial intelligence to gather information from the physical world?

A. Batteries

B. Sensors

C. Monitors

D. Speakers

2. Which of the following is NOT considered a sensor?

A. Camera

B. Microphone

C. GPS Receiver

D. Keyboard

3. Why is data important to AI?

A. It makes computers heavier.

B. It gives AI information to learn and make decisions.

C. It changes the color of software.

D. It slows down computers.

4. Which technology helps autonomous vehicles detect nearby objects?

A. Printer

B. Lidar

C. Flashlight

D. Calculator

5. Which statement best describes the AI Sensor Ecosystem?

A. A single computer program

B. A network of sensors collecting information for AI systems

C. A social media platform

D. A video game

True or False

6. _____ AI naturally sees the world the same way humans do.
7. _____ Sensors collect data that AI analyzes.
8. _____ Smartphones contain multiple sensors.
9. _____ Satellites can provide information to AI systems.
10. _____ Ethical use of data is important when developing AI systems.

Answer Key

Multiple Choice

1. **B**
2. **D**
3. **B**
4. **B**
5. **B**

True or False

6. **False**
7. **True**
8. **True**
9. **True**
10. **True**

Classroom Discussion

1. How would your daily life change if smartphones had no sensors?
2. Should AI be allowed to collect information everywhere? Why or why not?
3. What responsibilities do companies have when collecting sensor data?
4. How might AI sensors improve healthcare, transportation, or education?
5. As AI becomes more connected to everyday life, what skills do students need to become responsible users and future developers of AI?

Learn AI. Understand AI. Shape the Future.

— Susie Hala
IntelliGloss Press

Chapter 2

Why AI Cannot Learn Without Sensors

How Data Becomes Intelligence

Artificial intelligence is often praised for its ability to recognize faces, understand speech, recommend movies, drive vehicles, detect diseases, translate languages, and even generate artwork. These abilities may seem almost magical, but every AI system shares one important limitation: it cannot learn anything unless it first receives information. Intelligence begins with observation, and observation requires data. Without a continuous stream of information flowing into an AI system, even the world's most advanced computer would be unable to recognize patterns, solve problems, or make intelligent decisions. This simple truth explains why sensors are considered one of the most important foundations of artificial intelligence.

Imagine asking someone to identify an object while keeping their eyes completely closed. Without seeing, touching, or hearing anything about the object, they would simply be guessing. Human intelligence depends on information gathered through the five senses. The brain receives signals from the eyes, ears, skin, nose, and tongue before making decisions about the environment. Artificial intelligence works in a surprisingly similar way. Although AI does not possess biological senses, it relies on electronic sensors to gather information from the world. Cameras capture images, microphones detect sound, GPS receivers identify locations, radar measures distance, lidar creates three-dimensional maps, and temperature sensors monitor environmental conditions. These devices provide AI with the raw information it needs to begin learning.

One of the biggest misconceptions about artificial intelligence is the belief that AI automatically understands everything it sees. In reality, sensors do not understand information. They simply collect measurements. A digital camera does not recognize a stop sign. It only records millions of colored pixels arranged in a particular pattern. A microphone does not understand speech. It simply converts sound waves into electrical signals. A GPS receiver does not know that a vehicle is traveling to school or to work. It only calculates geographic coordinates. Sensors collect facts about the physical world, but artificial intelligence must interpret those facts before they become meaningful knowledge.

This distinction between **data** and **understanding** is one of the most important concepts in artificial intelligence. Data consists of individual pieces of information collected from sensors. These pieces of information may include numbers, images, sounds, temperatures, distances, locations, or movement. By themselves, these measurements have very little meaning. AI uses mathematical models, machine learning algorithms, and pattern recognition techniques to organize these measurements into useful knowledge. For example, thousands of individual pixels become the image of a pedestrian crossing the street. Tiny variations in sound waves become spoken words. Changes in heart rate measurements become indicators of physical activity or medical conditions. Artificial intelligence transforms raw observations into useful conclusions.

To understand this process more clearly, imagine assembling a giant jigsaw puzzle. Each puzzle piece represents one small piece of sensor data. Looking at a single puzzle piece tells you very little about the complete picture. However, as more pieces are connected together, a recognizable image begins to appear. Artificial intelligence works much the same way. A single camera frame provides only a moment in time. A single GPS reading only identifies one location. A single temperature measurement reveals only one environmental condition. AI combines thousands or even millions of these observations to discover patterns that humans might never notice. The larger the collection of high-quality data, the more accurate AI's understanding becomes.

Machine learning depends heavily on this continuous flow of information. During training, AI systems analyze enormous collections of data to identify relationships between different observations. A facial recognition system may study millions of photographs to learn the unique characteristics of human faces. A speech recognition system analyzes countless hours of recorded conversations to distinguish words and accents. A medical AI examines thousands of X-rays, MRI scans, and CT images to recognize signs of disease. Each additional example helps the AI improve its ability to make accurate predictions. This process resembles how students become better readers or musicians through practice. The more examples they experience, the stronger their understanding becomes.

The quality of sensor data is just as important as the quantity. Imagine trying to read a book through a dirty window or listening to a teacher while standing beside a noisy construction site. Poor-quality information makes learning much more difficult. Artificial intelligence faces the same challenge. Cameras with blurry images, faulty microphones, damaged sensors, or incomplete datasets can produce incorrect conclusions. This problem is known as **"garbage in, garbage out."** If poor-quality information enters an AI system, poor-quality decisions often follow. For this reason, engineers spend enormous amounts of time improving sensor accuracy, removing errors, and ensuring that AI systems receive reliable information.

Artificial intelligence rarely depends on a single type of sensor. Instead, modern AI systems combine information from many different sensors simultaneously. This process is called **sensor fusion**. Consider an autonomous vehicle driving through a busy city. Cameras identify traffic lights and road signs. Radar measures the distance to nearby vehicles. Lidar builds a three-dimensional map of the environment. GPS provides the vehicle's location. Accelerometers detect changes in speed and direction. By combining information from all these sensors, AI develops a much more complete understanding of its surroundings than any single sensor could provide. Humans unconsciously perform sensor fusion every day by combining sight, hearing, touch, balance, and other senses to understand the world around them.

Sensor fusion has transformed many industries beyond transportation. In healthcare, wearable devices monitor heart rate, blood oxygen levels, sleep patterns, and physical activity to help physicians monitor patients remotely. In agriculture, AI combines information from weather stations, soil moisture sensors, satellite imagery, and drone photography to help farmers improve crop production while conserving water and fertilizer. Manufacturing facilities use vibration sensors, pressure sensors, temperature sensors, and machine vision systems to predict equipment failures before they occur, reducing costly downtime. Environmental scientists combine satellite imagery, ocean sensors, weather stations, and wildlife tracking devices to better understand climate change and protect natural ecosystems. Each example demonstrates that AI becomes more effective when it receives information from multiple sources working together.

As the AI Sensor Ecosystem continues expanding across the world, another important challenge emerges: managing the enormous amount of data being collected. Every second, billions of sensors generate information. Self-driving vehicles can produce terabytes of data in a single day. Satellites continuously photograph Earth's surface. Smart cities monitor traffic flow, energy use, and environmental conditions. Smartphones collect location information, movement data, and communication signals. Artificial intelligence helps organize this overwhelming amount of information by filtering unnecessary details, identifying meaningful patterns, and presenting useful insights to people who must make decisions. Without AI, the sheer volume of sensor data would be impossible for humans to analyze efficiently.

Although sensors provide AI with extraordinary capabilities, they also introduce important ethical responsibilities. Every sensor that collects information raises questions about privacy, consent, cybersecurity, and fairness. Who should have access to data collected by smart devices? How long should information be stored? How can organizations protect sensitive personal information from cyberattacks? What happens if an AI system learns from inaccurate or biased data? Responsible AI development requires more than advanced technology. It requires thoughtful human decision-making that balances innovation with respect for individual rights and public trust.

Artificial intelligence is often compared to the human brain, but a more complete comparison includes the entire human body. The brain alone cannot understand the world without receiving information from the eyes, ears, skin, muscles, and nervous system. Likewise, artificial intelligence depends on its sensor ecosystem to gather the information necessary for learning and decision-making. Sensors provide observation. Data provides experience. Machine learning discovers patterns. Intelligence emerges from the successful combination of all these elements working together.

As you continue exploring this book, remember one important principle: **AI is only as intelligent as the information it receives.** Every breakthrough in artificial intelligence—from medical diagnosis and scientific discovery to autonomous transportation and robotics—begins with accurate data collected from reliable sensors. Understanding this relationship between sensors, data, and learning provides one of the strongest foundations for understanding how today's AI systems operate and how tomorrow's intelligent technologies will continue transforming our world.

Learn AI. Understand AI. Shape the Future.

— Susie Hala
IntelliGloss Press

Chapter 2 Summary

Chapter 2 explored why artificial intelligence cannot learn without sensors and why data is the foundation of every AI system. Unlike humans, who naturally gather information through their eyes, ears, skin, nose, and tongue, AI depends entirely on electronic sensors to observe the world around it. Cameras, microphones, GPS receivers, lidar, radar, temperature sensors, and many other devices collect information that AI analyzes to make decisions.

The chapter explained that sensors do not understand information—they simply collect measurements. Artificial intelligence transforms this raw data into useful knowledge through machine learning and pattern recognition. Readers learned the important difference between data, information, and intelligence, discovering that AI must analyze millions of pieces of information before it can recognize patterns and solve problems.

The chapter also introduced the concept of **sensor fusion**, where AI combines information from multiple sensors to develop a more complete understanding of its environment. Students explored real-world examples from autonomous vehicles, healthcare, agriculture, manufacturing, and environmental science, demonstrating how AI becomes more accurate when multiple sensors work together.

Finally, the chapter emphasized that high-quality data is essential for successful AI systems. Poor-quality or biased data can lead to incorrect decisions, highlighting the importance of accuracy, cybersecurity, ethics, and responsible AI development.

Reflection

Artificial intelligence is often admired for its ability to make intelligent decisions, but intelligence does not begin with algorithms. It begins with observation. Every AI system depends on sensors that collect information from the physical world before learning can take place. Understanding this relationship helps us realize that AI is not magical—it is built upon careful observation, reliable data, and continuous learning.

As technology continues to evolve, sensors will become even more advanced, collecting larger amounts of information than ever before. This growth creates tremendous opportunities to improve healthcare, transportation, education, environmental protection, and scientific research. However, it also increases our responsibility to use AI ethically, protect personal privacy, and ensure that the information used to train AI systems is accurate, fair, and trustworthy.

Learning how AI gathers information prepares us not only to use artificial intelligence wisely but also to become thoughtful designers, engineers, educators, and leaders who will shape the future of intelligent technologies.

Student Worksheet

Name: ______________________________

Part A – Vocabulary

Define each term in your own words.

1. Sensor

____

____

2. Sensor Fusion

____

____

3. Machine Learning

____

____

4. Raw Data

____

____

5. Pattern Recognition

Part B – Short Answer

1. Why can't AI learn without sensors?

2. Explain the difference between raw data and useful information.

3. What is sensor fusion, and why is it important?

4. List four industries that benefit from AI sensors.

5. Why is high-quality data important when training AI systems?

Part C – Critical Thinking

Imagine you are designing an AI-powered rescue robot for firefighters.

Write one paragraph describing:

- What sensors would the robot need?
- What information would each sensor collect?
- How would AI use that information to help save lives?

____

____

____

____

____

____

____

Chapter 2 Quiz

Multiple Choice

1. What is the primary purpose of a sensor?

A. Store electricity

B. Collect information from the environment

C. Increase internet speed

D. Display computer graphics

2. Which statement best describes raw data?

A. Final decisions made by AI

B. Information collected before AI analyzes it

C. A completed computer program

D. A finished report

3. What is sensor fusion?

A. Turning sensors off

B. Combining information from multiple sensors

C. Connecting two computers

D. Downloading software

4. Why is high-quality data important?

A. It makes computers heavier.

B. It helps AI make more accurate decisions.

C. It increases battery life.

D. It reduces internet speed.

5. Which technology combines cameras, lidar, radar, and GPS?

A. Calculator

B. Self-driving vehicle

C. Television

D. Printer

True or False

6. _____ AI understands information before sensors collect it.

7. _____ Sensors collect raw data.

8. _____ Machine learning finds patterns within data.

9. _____ Poor-quality data can reduce AI accuracy.

10. _____ Responsible AI includes protecting privacy and using trustworthy data.

Bonus Question

Imagine AI receives incorrect information from several sensors.

How might this affect its decisions?

Answer Key

Multiple Choice

1. **B** — Collect information from the environment
2. **B** — Information collected before AI analyzes it
3. **B** — Combining information from multiple sensors
4. **B** — It helps AI make more accurate decisions
5. **B** — Self-driving vehicle

True or False

6. **False**
7. **True**
8. **True**
9. **True**
10. **True**

Bonus Question (Sample Answer)

If AI receives incorrect or incomplete information from its sensors, it may make poor decisions because it is analyzing inaccurate data. This demonstrates the importance of reliable sensors, accurate data collection, and continuous system monitoring.

Classroom Discussion

1. Why is collecting accurate information just as important as building powerful AI algorithms?
2. How is AI learning similar to the way humans learn through their senses?
3. Can you think of examples where poor-quality data could create dangerous AI decisions?
4. Why do self-driving vehicles use multiple sensors instead of relying on only one camera?
5. As AI becomes more common in everyday life, what responsibilities do engineers, governments, businesses, and citizens have to ensure AI systems are fair, accurate, and trustworthy?

Learn AI. Understand AI. Shape the Future.

— Susie Hala
IntelliGloss Press

Chapter 3

AI's Eyes: Cameras, Computer Vision, and Image Recognition

Imagine waking up one morning and discovering that you could no longer see. You could still hear voices, feel the warmth of the sun on your skin, smell breakfast cooking in the kitchen, and recognize familiar sounds around you. However, something very important would be missing. Without vision, recognizing faces, reading a book, driving a car, catching a ball, or even walking safely through a crowded hallway would become much more difficult. Vision provides an extraordinary amount of information that allows the human brain to understand the world almost instantly. Every second, your eyes continuously collect light, colors, shapes, movement, distance, and depth, sending billions of pieces of information to your brain for interpretation. Although most people never think about this process, vision is one of the most remarkable biological systems ever developed.

Artificial intelligence faces a similar challenge. AI cannot naturally see the world because it does not have biological eyes or a brain. A computer sitting on a desk has no understanding of people, buildings, animals, traffic signs, or written words unless information is provided to it. Engineers quickly realized that if they wanted machines to perform tasks requiring visual understanding, they first had to give computers an artificial way to observe the world. This challenge led to the development of one of the most important fields in modern artificial intelligence: **computer vision**.

Computer vision is the branch of AI that allows machines to collect visual information through cameras and interpret that information in meaningful ways. It combines digital cameras, image sensors, powerful computers, mathematical algorithms, and machine learning models to recognize objects, identify people, inspect products, interpret medical images, analyze satellite photographs, and perform thousands of other tasks that once required human eyesight. Every time your smartphone unlocks by recognizing your face, every time a self-driving vehicle identifies a stop sign, or every time doctors use AI to help detect cancer in an X-ray, computer vision is working behind the scenes.

Although computer vision is often described as giving AI the ability to "see," it is important to understand that AI does not see the world the way humans do. Human vision is a biological process developed over millions of years through evolution. Light enters the eye through the cornea and pupil before reaching the retina, a thin layer containing millions of specialized cells called rods and cones. These cells convert light into electrical signals that travel through the optic nerve to the brain. The brain then combines those signals with memory, experience, and context, allowing you to recognize a friend's face, identify a bicycle, or read the words on this page almost effortlessly.

Artificial intelligence follows a different process. Instead of eyes, AI uses digital cameras equipped with electronic image sensors. These sensors perform a role similar to the retina in the human eye, but they do so electronically rather than biologically. When light enters a camera through its lens, it strikes millions of tiny light-sensitive elements located on the image sensor. Each element measures the amount of light reaching it and converts that measurement into a digital value. These millions of measurements become the digital photograph that the computer receives. Unlike humans, however, the computer has no natural understanding of what those measurements represent. To the computer, the image initially appears as nothing more than enormous collections of numbers waiting to be analyzed.

This idea surprises many students because photographs appear simple to human observers. Looking at a family picture, you immediately recognize parents, children, clothing, trees, pets, and smiles without consciously thinking about the process. Your brain has spent your entire life learning how to recognize visual patterns. Artificial intelligence must learn these same patterns through training. Before AI can identify a cat, it may need to analyze hundreds of thousands or even millions of cat photographs. During training, machine learning algorithms compare countless examples, gradually discovering the characteristics that make cats different from dogs, rabbits, birds, or other animals. Over time, the AI develops mathematical models that allow it to recognize similar patterns in new images it has never seen before.

The smallest building block of every digital image is called a **pixel**, short for "picture element." A pixel is a tiny square that stores information about color and brightness. Individually, a single pixel has almost no meaning. However, when millions of pixels are arranged together, they create detailed photographs that humans and AI systems can analyze. Consider a high-resolution smartphone camera capable of capturing twelve million pixels in a single photograph. Each pixel records only a tiny amount of information, but together they produce an image detailed enough for AI to recognize faces, read text, detect road signs, inspect products, or identify diseases from medical scans.

One helpful way to understand pixels is to imagine creating a large mural using colored ceramic tiles. Looking closely at one tile reveals only a single color. Stepping back several feet allows thousands of tiles to combine into a beautiful image. Digital photographs work the same way. Each pixel contributes one small piece of information, but millions of pixels together create the complete picture. Artificial intelligence examines these individual pixels mathematically, measuring changes in color, brightness, edges, textures, and shapes that humans often overlook. Instead of seeing a smiling face, the AI initially detects numerical patterns representing contrasts, lines, curves, and color variations. Only after extensive training does the AI learn that these mathematical patterns correspond to human faces.

The quality of an image greatly influences how accurately AI performs its work. High-resolution cameras capture more pixels, providing greater detail for analysis. Better lighting improves image clarity, while proper focus helps preserve important visual features. Conversely, poor lighting, motion blur, heavy rain, fog, snow, shadows, or damaged camera lenses may reduce image quality and make accurate recognition more difficult. Humans experience similar challenges. Reading a street sign during a heavy rainstorm or recognizing a friend standing in deep shadows is more difficult because less visual information reaches our eyes. Computer vision systems face many of these same obstacles and must often compensate using sophisticated algorithms designed to improve image quality before analysis begins.

As camera technology continues to improve, artificial intelligence gains access to increasingly detailed visual information. Modern AI systems analyze photographs measured not only in millions of pixels but also in multiple wavelengths of light that humans cannot naturally perceive. Infrared cameras reveal heat patterns invisible to the human eye. Thermal imaging allows firefighters to locate people trapped inside smoke-filled buildings. Satellite imaging detects changes in forests, oceans, farmland, and cities from hundreds of miles above Earth. Medical imaging systems reveal structures hidden beneath human skin. These technologies demonstrate that computer vision is not simply copying human eyesight—it is extending vision beyond normal human limitations.

One of the greatest achievements of computer vision is its ability to transform raw images into useful knowledge. A camera may capture millions of pixels, but artificial intelligence organizes those pixels into meaningful information that supports decision-making. In the next section of this chapter, you will discover how AI moves beyond simply seeing images to identifying objects, recognizing faces, reading printed text, assisting physicians in diagnosing diseases, guiding autonomous vehicles safely through traffic, monitoring crops from space, and helping scientists better understand our rapidly changing world. As you continue learning, you will discover that cameras do far more than take photographs—they serve as the eyes of intelligent machines that are reshaping nearly every aspect of modern life.

Learn AI. Understand AI. Shape the Future.

— Susie Hala
IntelliGloss Press

Chapter 3 Summary

Chapter 3 introduced **computer vision**, the branch of artificial intelligence that enables machines to collect and interpret visual information. Since AI does not have biological eyes like humans, it relies on digital cameras and image sensors to observe the world. Cameras capture light from the environment and convert it into digital information that computers can process. Artificial intelligence then analyzes this information to recognize patterns, identify objects, and make intelligent decisions.

The chapter explained the similarities and differences between human vision and computer vision. Human eyes naturally send visual information to the brain, where years of experience help us recognize people, objects, and environments. AI follows a different process. It receives digital images from cameras, converts those images into numerical data, and uses machine learning algorithms to identify patterns that correspond to specific objects or situations.

Students also learned about **pixels**, the tiny picture elements that form every digital image. Although a single pixel contains very little information, millions of pixels work together to create detailed photographs. Artificial intelligence examines these pixels mathematically to identify colors, edges, shapes, textures, and patterns that help determine what an image contains.

The chapter emphasized that image quality plays an important role in AI accuracy. Good lighting, clear focus, and high-resolution images improve computer vision performance, while poor lighting, fog, motion blur, or damaged cameras can reduce accuracy. Readers also discovered that modern computer vision extends beyond normal human eyesight by using infrared cameras, thermal imaging, satellite imaging, and other technologies capable of detecting information invisible to the human eye.

Finally, the chapter demonstrated that computer vision is becoming one of the most important technologies in artificial intelligence. It powers facial recognition, autonomous vehicles, medical diagnosis, robotics, manufacturing, agriculture, environmental monitoring, and countless other applications that continue transforming industries around the world.

Reflection

Vision is one of humanity's greatest abilities because it allows us to understand our surroundings almost instantly. Artificial intelligence must achieve this same goal through cameras, sensors, mathematics, and machine learning. Computer vision demonstrates that intelligence is not simply about collecting information—it is about interpreting information correctly.

As computer vision becomes increasingly powerful, society benefits from safer transportation, improved medical diagnosis, better manufacturing, environmental protection, and scientific discovery. However, these advancements also require thoughtful discussions about privacy, fairness, security, and responsible technology use.

Understanding computer vision helps us appreciate both the remarkable achievements of artificial intelligence and the responsibilities that come with developing machines capable of observing the world around them.

Student Worksheet

Name: ____

Part A – Vocabulary

Define each vocabulary word using your own words.

1. Computer Vision

2. Pixel

3. Image Sensor

4. Digital Image

5. Pattern Recognition

Part B – Short Answer

1. Why can't artificial intelligence naturally see the world?

2. Explain how a camera helps AI collect information.

3. What is a pixel, and why is it important?

4. Describe two differences between human vision and computer vision.

5. Why does image quality affect AI performance?

Part C – Critical Thinking

Imagine you have been hired to design an AI vision system for a hospital.

Write one paragraph explaining:

- What cameras or imaging devices would be used?
- How would AI analyze the images?
- How could computer vision help doctors provide better patient care?

Chapter 3 Quiz

Multiple Choice

1. What gives artificial intelligence the ability to collect visual information?

A. Speakers

B. Digital cameras

C. Batteries

D. Hard drives

2. What does a camera convert into digital information?

A. Electricity

B. Light

C. Heat

D. Sound

3. What is the smallest unit of a digital image?

A. Sensor

B. Pixel

C. Algorithm

D. Database

4. Why does AI analyze millions of pixels?

A. To increase battery life

B. To recognize patterns and identify objects

C. To make cameras larger

D. To store music

5. Which technology allows AI to see heat that humans cannot?

A. GPS

B. Infrared and thermal imaging

C. Bluetooth

D. Wi-Fi

True or False

6. _____ AI naturally sees exactly like humans.

7. _____ Cameras collect images before AI analyzes them.

8. _____ Better image quality usually improves AI accuracy.

9. _____ Computer vision is used in healthcare and autonomous vehicles.

10. _____ AI can analyze images collected by satellites.

Answer Key

Multiple Choice

1. **B** — Digital cameras
2. **B** — Light
3. **B** — Pixel
4. **B** — To recognize patterns and identify objects
5. **B** — Infrared and thermal imaging

True or False

6. **False**
7. **True**
8. **True**
9. **True**
10. **True**

Bonus Question

Imagine AI cameras are installed throughout a smart city.

Describe two benefits and two challenges of using computer vision in public places.

Sample Answer:

Benefits may include improving traffic safety, helping emergency responders, reducing accidents, locating missing persons, and improving public services. Challenges include protecting personal privacy, preventing unauthorized surveillance, securing collected data, and ensuring AI systems make fair and unbiased decisions.

Classroom Discussion

1. Why is computer vision considered one of the most important technologies in artificial intelligence?
2. How is human vision different from computer vision?
3. Why must AI be trained using thousands or even millions of images?
4. How can computer vision improve healthcare, agriculture, transportation, and environmental protection?
5. As AI cameras become more common in everyday life, how can society balance innovation, privacy, security, and ethical responsibility?

Key Takeaways

After completing this chapter, you should be able to:

- Explain why cameras serve as the "eyes" of artificial intelligence.
- Describe how light becomes digital information.
- Explain the role of pixels in creating digital images.
- Compare human vision with computer vision.
- Understand why image quality affects AI performance.
- Recognize how computer vision is transforming industries around the world.
- Appreciate the ethical responsibilities associated with AI systems that can observe and interpret the physical world.

Learn AI. Understand AI. Shape the Future.

— Susie Hala
IntelliGloss Press

Chapter 4

AI's Ears: Microphones, Sound Detection, and Speech Recognition

Imagine trying to live your entire life without the ability to hear. You could still see the world around you, but conversations would become silent, music would lose its melody, emergency sirens would go unnoticed, and the voices of family and friends would no longer reach your ears. Hearing is one of the most important human senses because it allows us to communicate, recognize danger, enjoy music, learn languages, and understand emotions through tone of voice. Every day, our ears collect thousands of sounds that our brains organize into meaningful information. Although we rarely think about this remarkable process, hearing plays an essential role in how we learn and interact with the world.

Artificial intelligence faces the same challenge. After giving AI the ability to see through cameras and computer vision, engineers realized that intelligent machines also needed the ability to hear. A robot working inside a hospital should recognize when someone calls for help. A virtual assistant should understand spoken questions. A self-driving vehicle should detect the siren of an approaching ambulance. A smart home should respond when someone asks it to turn on the lights. None of these tasks would be possible if AI could only see. Machines also needed ears.

Unlike humans, artificial intelligence does not have biological ears. Instead, AI depends on **microphones** and other sound sensors to collect audio information from the environment. Microphones serve as the ears of artificial intelligence by detecting tiny vibrations traveling through the air. Every sound we hear begins as a vibration. When a person speaks, vocal cords vibrate rapidly, creating pressure waves that travel through the atmosphere. These invisible sound waves eventually reach a microphone, which converts them into electrical signals that computers can process. Artificial intelligence then analyzes those signals to determine what was said, who spoke, and sometimes even how the speaker feels.

Understanding how microphones work helps us appreciate one of the most remarkable achievements of modern engineering. A microphone does not understand words, recognize music, or interpret emotions. Its only responsibility is to detect changes in air pressure caused by sound waves. Inside the microphone is a very thin diaphragm that vibrates whenever sound reaches it. These tiny vibrations are converted into electrical signals and then into digital data. The computer receives this information as millions of numerical values representing the loudness, timing, and frequency of each sound. Just as a digital camera converts light into numbers, a microphone converts sound into numbers. Artificial intelligence must then transform those numbers into meaningful information.

Humans perform this process naturally. When someone says, "Good morning," your ears capture the sound waves, and your brain instantly recognizes the words, identifies the speaker, understands the language, and often interprets the speaker's emotional tone. Artificial intelligence must learn each of these abilities separately. Engineers train AI using enormous collections of recorded speech representing different languages, accents, ages, speaking speeds, and environments. During training, machine learning algorithms gradually discover patterns within spoken language. Over time, AI becomes increasingly accurate at recognizing words, separating different speakers, and understanding spoken commands.

One of the most important applications of AI hearing is **Automatic Speech Recognition (ASR)**. Speech recognition allows computers to convert spoken language into written text. Millions of people use this technology every day without realizing how complex the process truly is. When someone speaks into a smartphone, AI must first separate the speaker's voice from background noise. Next, it divides continuous speech into individual sounds known as phonemes, the smallest units of spoken language. These phonemes are combined into words, words become sentences, and sentences are analyzed to determine their meaning. All of this often happens in less than a second, creating the impression that the computer naturally understands human speech.

Speech recognition has transformed education, healthcare, business, and everyday life. Students can dictate essays using voice typing software. Physicians record patient notes more efficiently through medical dictation systems. Businesses automatically transcribe meetings and interviews. Journalists convert recorded conversations into searchable text within minutes. Individuals with physical disabilities use voice commands to operate computers, smartphones, and household devices more independently. These examples demonstrate how AI hearing has become an important tool for improving accessibility and productivity.

Artificial intelligence can also recognize sounds that are not words. This field is known as **audio event detection**. Instead of identifying speech, AI learns to recognize environmental sounds such as breaking glass, barking dogs, crying babies, smoke alarms, gunshots, machinery failures, or emergency sirens. Smart security systems can alert homeowners when unusual sounds occur inside a building. Hospitals monitor patient rooms for signs of distress. Industrial facilities detect abnormal machine sounds that may indicate equipment problems before expensive failures occur. Wildlife researchers use AI to identify bird species by analyzing recorded songs deep within forests. In each case, AI transforms ordinary sound into valuable information.

Modern AI systems often go one step further by attempting to recognize **emotion** in speech. Human communication involves much more than words alone. Tone of voice, speaking speed, volume, pauses, and pitch often reveal whether someone is happy, frightened, angry, excited, or uncertain. Researchers have developed AI models capable of analyzing these vocal characteristics to estimate emotional states. Customer service organizations may use these systems to identify frustrated callers. Healthcare professionals are exploring whether changes in speech patterns can help identify depression, neurological disorders, or cognitive decline. Although emotional recognition technology continues to improve, researchers also recognize that emotions are highly personal and culturally influenced, making this area one of the most challenging fields within artificial intelligence.

AI hearing is becoming increasingly important in robotics. Imagine a humanoid robot working alongside nurses in a hospital. Patients may ask for water, request assistance, or report discomfort. The robot must hear these requests accurately before deciding how to respond. Delivery robots operating inside airports or shopping centers must recognize spoken questions from travelers. Industrial robots working beside human employees may receive verbal instructions while simultaneously monitoring machinery sounds for signs of equipment failure. These examples demonstrate that hearing allows robots to interact with people more naturally and safely.

However, hearing presents challenges that vision alone does not. Background conversations, wind, traffic, music, echoes, and poor-quality microphones can interfere with accurate speech recognition. Different languages, accents, dialects, and speaking styles add additional complexity. Humans often understand incomplete sentences because they rely on experience and context. AI must learn these abilities through enormous amounts of training data and increasingly sophisticated language models. Engineers continue improving these systems so AI can communicate more naturally while reducing misunderstandings.

As microphones become smaller and more powerful, AI hearing is expanding into nearly every aspect of modern life. Smart speakers respond to voice commands from across a room. Smartphones translate conversations between different languages in real time. Vehicles recognize spoken navigation requests while drivers keep their hands on the steering wheel. Emergency dispatch centers use AI to prioritize urgent calls. Scientific researchers monitor endangered wildlife by listening to forests, oceans, and wetlands. Even spacecraft exploring distant planets rely on sensitive sensors that analyze vibrations and acoustic signals in environments very different from Earth.

With these remarkable capabilities come important ethical responsibilities. Devices that continuously listen for voice commands also raise legitimate questions about privacy and security. Who owns voice recordings? How long should they be stored? Can conversations be protected from unauthorized access? How can organizations ensure AI systems fairly understand different accents and languages without introducing bias? Responsible AI development requires balancing technological innovation with respect for personal privacy, transparency, and informed consent.

Computer vision gave artificial intelligence the ability to observe the world through images. Microphones and sound recognition now allow AI to listen, communicate, and better understand human activity. Together, vision and hearing create a far richer understanding of the environment than either sense could provide alone. In the chapters ahead, you will discover that as AI gains additional artificial senses, intelligent machines become increasingly capable of assisting people in solving complex problems while opening new opportunities for education, healthcare, science, engineering, and society.

Learn AI. Understand AI. Shape the Future.

— Susie Hala
IntelliGloss Press

Chapter 4 Summary

Chapter 4 explored how artificial intelligence gains the ability to hear through microphones, sound sensors, and speech recognition technologies. Just as cameras serve as the eyes of AI, microphones serve as its ears by collecting sound waves from the surrounding environment and converting them into digital information that computers can analyze.

The chapter explained that sound begins as vibrations traveling through the air. Microphones detect these vibrations and convert them into electrical signals, which are then transformed into digital data. Artificial intelligence analyzes this data to recognize speech, identify sounds, interpret spoken commands, and detect important events occurring in the environment.

Students learned that AI hearing involves much more than simply recognizing words. AI must separate speech from background noise, identify different speakers, recognize accents and languages, and sometimes even estimate emotions by analyzing changes in tone, pitch, and speaking patterns. These abilities are made possible through machine learning, where AI is trained using enormous collections of recorded speech and environmental sounds.

The chapter also introduced Automatic Speech Recognition (ASR), which allows computers to convert spoken language into written text. Students discovered how speech recognition has improved education, healthcare, business, accessibility, robotics, customer service, and everyday communication.

Finally, the chapter discussed the ethical challenges associated with AI hearing. As voice-controlled devices become increasingly common, society must carefully consider issues involving privacy, data security, fairness, informed consent, and responsible use of voice recordings. Understanding how AI hears helps students appreciate one of the most important technologies that allows humans and intelligent machines to communicate naturally.

Reflection

Communication is one of humanity's greatest strengths. Every conversation, lesson, emergency call, and musical performance depends on our ability to hear and understand sound. Artificial intelligence has made remarkable progress in developing similar abilities through microphones, speech recognition, and sound analysis.

Learning how AI hears reminds us that communication is much more than recognizing words. Context, tone, emotion, and background sounds all contribute to understanding what someone is trying to communicate. As AI continues improving its ability to interact with people, engineers and society must ensure that these systems respect privacy, protect personal information, and treat all users fairly regardless of language, accent, or culture.

Understanding AI hearing prepares students to become informed users, future developers, and responsible leaders who recognize both the benefits and responsibilities of intelligent communication technologies.

Student Worksheet

Name: ______________________________

Part A – Vocabulary

Define each term using your own words.

1. Microphone

____

____

2. Sound Wave

____

____

3. Automatic Speech Recognition (ASR)

____

____

4. Audio Event Detection

____

____

5. Machine Learning

____

____

____

Part B – Short Answer

1. Why are microphones considered the "ears" of artificial intelligence?

____

____

____

2. Explain how sound becomes digital information.

3. What is Automatic Speech Recognition, and how is it used?

4. Give four examples of industries that benefit from AI hearing.

5. Why is privacy important when AI systems listen to human speech?

Part C – Critical Thinking

Imagine your school installs an AI-powered emergency communication system.

Write one paragraph explaining:

- What sounds should AI recognize?
- How could the system improve school safety?
- What privacy protections should be included?

Chapter 4 Quiz

Multiple Choice

1. Which device serves as the ears of artificial intelligence?

A. Camera

B. Microphone

C. GPS

D. Keyboard

2. What does a microphone detect?

A. Light

B. Sound waves

C. Heat

D. Electricity

3. What does Automatic Speech Recognition (ASR) do?

A. Creates videos

B. Converts spoken language into written text

C. Builds robots

D. Detects internet connections

4. Which of the following is an example of audio event detection?

A. Reading a book

B. Detecting a smoke alarm

C. Measuring temperature

D. Printing a document

5. Why does AI require large collections of recorded speech during training?

A. To increase internet speed

B. To learn different voices, accents, and speaking patterns

C. To improve battery life

D. To create louder speakers

True or False

6. _____ AI naturally understands human language without training.

7. _____ Sound begins as vibrations traveling through the air.

8. _____ AI can recognize environmental sounds as well as speech.

9. _____ Speech recognition is used in healthcare and education.

10. _____ Responsible AI hearing includes protecting people's privacy.

Answer Key

Multiple Choice

1. **B** — Microphone
2. **B** — Sound waves
3. **B** — Converts spoken language into written text
4. **B** — Detecting a smoke alarm
5. **B** — To learn different voices, accents, and speaking patterns

True or False

6. **False**
7. **True**
8. **True**

9. **True**
10. **True**

Bonus Question

Describe one way AI hearing could improve life for people with disabilities.

Sample Answer:

AI hearing can help people with hearing impairments by providing real-time speech-to-text captions during conversations, classroom instruction, meetings, or public events. It can also assist individuals with limited mobility by allowing them to control computers, smartphones, and smart home devices using voice commands.

Classroom Discussion

1. Why is hearing just as important as vision for artificial intelligence?
2. How is AI hearing different from human hearing?
3. Why must AI learn from many different languages, accents, and speaking styles?
4. What are some benefits and risks of voice-controlled AI devices?
5. As AI becomes better at understanding speech, how can society protect privacy while still benefiting from intelligent communication technologies?

Key Takeaways

After completing this chapter, you should be able to:

- Explain how microphones collect sound for artificial intelligence.
- Describe how sound waves become digital information.
- Understand how Automatic Speech Recognition converts speech into text.
- Explain how AI recognizes environmental sounds and spoken language.
- Identify real-world applications of AI hearing in healthcare, education, business, robotics, and public safety.
- Recognize the ethical responsibilities associated with AI listening technologies.
- Understand why hearing is one of the essential artificial senses that allows AI to interact naturally with people and its environment.

Learn AI. Understand AI. Shape the Future.

— Susie Hala
IntelliGloss Press

Chapter 5

AI's Sense of Touch: Pressure, Force, and Tactile Sensors

Imagine trying to pick up a fragile glass of water while wearing thick gloves that completely block your sense of touch. You could still see the glass sitting on the table, but without feeling it, you would not know whether you were squeezing too hard or too softly. Grip the glass too tightly, and it might break. Hold it too loosely, and it could slip from your hand and fall to the floor. Something that normally requires almost no thought would suddenly become much more difficult. This simple example demonstrates why the sense of touch is essential to everyday life. Touch allows us to interact safely with the physical world by helping us measure pressure, texture, temperature, weight, movement, and balance. Every time you shake someone's hand, write with a pencil, open a door, or hold a baby, your sense of touch quietly helps your brain make thousands of tiny adjustments without you even realizing it.

Artificial intelligence faces a similar challenge. Cameras allow AI to see, and microphones allow AI to hear, but seeing and hearing alone are not enough when machines must physically interact with people or objects. A robot working in a hospital cannot safely hand a patient a glass of water if it cannot determine how firmly it is holding the cup. A robotic arm assembling electronic components cannot install delicate computer chips if it cannot detect the amount of pressure being applied. An autonomous warehouse robot cannot safely move packages if it cannot determine whether an object is slipping from its mechanical gripper. Engineers quickly realized that intelligent machines also needed an artificial sense of touch. This need led to the development of **tactile sensors**, pressure sensors, force sensors, and many other technologies that allow AI to physically interact with its surroundings.

Unlike humans, robots do not have skin filled with millions of nerve endings. Human skin contains specialized sensory receptors that constantly send information to the brain about pressure, temperature, vibration, pain, and movement. These receptors allow people to recognize whether an object feels smooth or rough, hot or cold, soft or hard. Artificial intelligence cannot naturally experience these sensations. Instead, engineers design electronic sensors that measure physical contact and convert these measurements into digital information. Artificial intelligence analyzes this information and determines how to respond appropriately. Although robots do not actually "feel" in the human sense, tactile sensors allow them to detect physical interactions with remarkable precision.

One of the most common touch technologies used in AI is the **pressure sensor**. A pressure sensor measures the amount of force being applied to an object or surface. Every time you press a key on your computer keyboard, touch your smartphone screen, or step onto a digital scale, pressure sensors are collecting information. In robotics, pressure sensors allow machines to determine whether they are gripping an object too tightly or too gently. Industrial robots assembling automobiles use pressure sensors to install components with extreme precision. Medical robots performing delicate surgical procedures rely on pressure measurements to avoid damaging surrounding tissue. Even modern elevators use pressure-sensitive systems to determine whether passengers are blocking the closing doors.

Closely related to pressure sensing is **force sensing**. Although pressure and force are connected, they measure different aspects of physical interaction. Force sensors determine how much pushing, pulling, lifting, twisting, or compression is being applied during movement. Imagine lifting a heavy backpack compared to picking up an empty notebook. Your muscles automatically adjust because your nervous system continuously measures the amount of force required. Robots must perform similar calculations. A robotic warehouse worker lifting a heavy shipping box requires much more force than when moving a lightweight envelope. AI uses force sensors to continuously monitor these differences and adjust motor movements accordingly.

Touch also allows humans to recognize the texture of objects. Without looking, most people can easily distinguish between sandpaper, silk, wood, glass, rubber, or metal simply by running their fingers across the surface. Engineers have developed advanced tactile sensors capable of detecting similar surface characteristics. These sensors measure tiny differences in friction, vibration, and surface resistance. Manufacturing companies use this technology to inspect products for defects that may be invisible to cameras alone. Agricultural robots use tactile sensing to determine whether fruit has ripened enough for harvesting without damaging the crop. Food processing systems measure texture to ensure product quality before packaging. Through these technologies, AI expands beyond simple vision and begins interacting with the physical properties of materials.

Temperature sensing adds another important dimension to artificial touch. Human skin constantly monitors temperature to help protect the body from burns, frostbite, and environmental hazards. Artificial intelligence also depends on temperature sensors in many industries. Manufacturing equipment monitors engine temperatures to prevent overheating. Smart buildings automatically adjust heating and cooling systems based on temperature measurements. Medical devices continuously monitor patient body temperature during surgery and intensive care. Environmental scientists place temperature sensors in oceans, forests, and polar regions to study climate change. Although temperature sensors do not provide the emotional experience of feeling warmth or cold, they allow AI to detect thermal conditions with extraordinary accuracy.

One of the most exciting developments in robotics is the creation of robotic hands capable of performing delicate tasks that once required human dexterity. Building such systems has proven extremely difficult because the human hand contains dozens of joints, muscles, tendons, and thousands of sensory receptors working together. When you pick up an egg, your fingers automatically adjust pressure to avoid crushing the shell while still maintaining a secure grip. Engineers have spent decades studying this remarkable biological system while developing robotic hands equipped with pressure sensors, force sensors, and tactile feedback. These robotic systems can now sort fragile fruits, assemble miniature electronic devices, assist surgeons during operations, and handle laboratory samples with incredible precision. Each improvement brings robots closer to safely interacting with people and delicate objects.

Artificial touch has also transformed the field of **prosthetic limbs**. Traditional prosthetic arms allowed users to perform limited movements, but they provided little or no sensory feedback. Modern AI-powered prosthetic limbs are becoming increasingly sophisticated. Some systems contain sensors that measure pressure, grip strength, and movement while using artificial intelligence to interpret the user's intentions. Researchers are even developing technologies that return limited sensory information to the user's nervous system, allowing individuals to experience a basic sense of touch through advanced prosthetic devices. Although these technologies continue to evolve, they represent one of the most inspiring examples of AI improving human lives.

As robots become more common in hospitals, schools, businesses, factories, and homes, touch becomes increasingly important for safety. Imagine a service robot delivering medicine to a patient or helping an elderly person stand up from a chair. The robot must carefully monitor every movement to avoid applying excessive force that could cause injury. Engineers therefore design AI systems that constantly monitor tactile information while immediately stopping movement if unexpected resistance or unsafe conditions are detected. These safety systems allow humans and robots to work together more confidently in shared environments.

Although artificial touch has advanced significantly, it still differs greatly from human touch. Humans instantly combine touch with vision, hearing, balance, memory, and experience. When you touch a hot pan, you immediately recognize danger and pull your hand away without consciously thinking. AI performs similar actions through programmed safety systems and machine learning, but it does not experience pain or discomfort. Instead, sensors simply report measurements that algorithms interpret according to predefined rules or learned patterns. This distinction reminds us that AI simulates aspects of human perception without actually possessing human consciousness or feelings.

Researchers continue exploring one of the most fascinating frontiers in robotics: **electronic skin**, often called **e-skin**. Electronic skin consists of flexible materials containing thousands of tiny sensors distributed across a robotic surface. Much like human skin, e-skin can detect pressure, stretching, temperature, and physical contact across large areas. Scientists hope these technologies will improve humanoid robots, advanced prosthetics, wearable healthcare devices, and future space exploration systems. Although electronic skin remains an active area of research, it represents another step toward creating machines capable of interacting more naturally with the physical world.

Computer vision gave artificial intelligence the ability to observe. Microphones gave AI the ability to listen and communicate. Tactile sensors now provide the ability to interact physically with people and objects. As additional artificial senses continue to develop, AI systems become more capable of assisting humanity in healthcare, manufacturing, education, scientific research, disaster response, environmental protection, and countless other fields. Understanding how AI senses touch helps us appreciate that intelligence is not built from algorithms alone. It is created by combining multiple streams of information that allow machines to safely perceive and respond to the world around them.

Learn AI. Understand AI. Shape the Future.

— Susie Hala
IntelliGloss Press

Chapter 5 Summary

Chapter 5 introduced the concept of **AI's sense of touch**, explaining how artificial intelligence uses pressure, force, and tactile sensors to safely interact with the physical world. Unlike humans, who naturally experience touch through millions of nerve endings in their skin, AI relies on electronic sensors that detect physical contact and convert it into digital information.

The chapter explained that cameras and microphones allow AI to see and hear, but robots also need to physically interact with objects. Pressure sensors help robots determine how firmly they are gripping an object, while force sensors measure pushing, pulling, lifting, and twisting movements. These sensors allow AI to safely perform delicate tasks that require precision and control.

Students learned that tactile sensors can detect surface characteristics such as texture, pressure, vibration, and contact. These technologies are widely used in manufacturing, healthcare, agriculture, robotics, prosthetic limbs, and warehouse automation. AI uses this information to make intelligent adjustments while handling fragile objects, assisting surgeons, harvesting crops, or helping people with disabilities.

The chapter also introduced electronic skin, or **e-skin**, an emerging technology designed to give robots a more advanced sense of touch. Researchers hope e-skin will improve humanoid robots, prosthetic devices, wearable healthcare technologies, and future space exploration systems.

Finally, the chapter emphasized that although AI can measure physical contact with extraordinary accuracy, it does not actually experience feelings or pain. Instead, it interprets sensor data using mathematical models and machine learning. As AI continues to develop more advanced artificial senses, engineers must ensure these systems remain safe, reliable, ethical, and beneficial to society.

Reflection

Touch is one of the most important human senses because it allows us to safely interact with the physical world. Every object we hold, every handshake we give, and every task we perform depends on our ability to sense pressure, temperature, texture, and movement. Artificial intelligence must develop similar abilities if robots are to safely assist people in homes, hospitals, factories, and public spaces.

Understanding AI's sense of touch reminds us that intelligence is not simply about solving mathematical problems. Intelligent machines must also interact safely with people and their environment. As robotic technologies continue advancing, engineers must design systems that combine accuracy, safety, and ethical responsibility. Developing AI that can safely touch and assist humans requires not only technological innovation but also careful consideration of trust, privacy, and human well-being.

Student Worksheet

Name: ______________________________

Part A – Vocabulary

Define each term using your own words.

1. Tactile Sensor

____

____

2. Pressure Sensor

____

____

3. Force Sensor

____

____

4. Electronic Skin (E-Skin)

____

____

5. Prosthetic Limb

____

____

____

Part B – Short Answer

1. Why does artificial intelligence need a sense of touch?

____

____

____

2. Explain the difference between pressure sensors and force sensors.

____

____

____

3. How do tactile sensors help robots handle fragile objects?

4. Give four examples of industries that use AI touch sensors.

5. Why is safety important when robots physically interact with people?

Part C – Critical Thinking

Imagine you are designing a robotic assistant for a children's hospital.

Write one paragraph explaining:

- What touch sensors would the robot need?
- How would those sensors help the robot safely interact with patients?
- What safety features would you include?

Chapter 5 Quiz

Multiple Choice

1. Which type of sensor allows AI to detect physical contact?

A. GPS

B. Tactile Sensor

C. Camera

D. Satellite

2. What does a pressure sensor measure?

A. Internet speed

B. The amount of pressure applied to an object

C. Sound waves

D. Light intensity

3. Which technology is designed to imitate human skin?

A. Fiber optics

B. Electronic Skin (E-Skin)

C. Bluetooth

D. Radar

4. Which profession benefits from AI-powered robotic surgery?

A. Farmers

B. Surgeons

C. Pilots

D. Architects

5. Why do robots use force sensors?

A. To measure pushing, pulling, lifting, and gripping forces

B. To improve internet connections

C. To increase battery size

D. To store photographs

True or False

6. _____ AI naturally experiences pain like humans.

7. _____ Pressure sensors help robots control how firmly they hold objects.

8. _____ Electronic skin is being researched to improve robotic touch.

9. _____ Touch sensors are used in healthcare and manufacturing.

10. _____ Responsible AI includes designing robots that can safely interact with people.

Answer Key

Multiple Choice

1. **B** — Tactile Sensor
2. **B** — The amount of pressure applied to an object
3. **B** — Electronic Skin (E-Skin)
4. **B** — Surgeons
5. **A** — To measure pushing, pulling, lifting, and gripping forces

True or False

6. **False**
7. **True**
8. **True**
9. **True**
10. **True**

Bonus Question

Imagine that future robots are equipped with electronic skin that closely imitates human touch.

What advantages could this technology provide, and what ethical concerns should society consider before using it widely?

Sample Answer:

Electronic skin could help robots safely assist elderly individuals, support medical rehabilitation, improve prosthetic limbs, and perform delicate manufacturing tasks. However, society should also consider privacy, safety, cybersecurity, human trust, and ensuring that robots remain tools designed to assist rather than replace meaningful human interaction.

Classroom Discussion

1. Why is the sense of touch just as important as vision and hearing for intelligent robots?
2. How do tactile sensors make robotic systems safer?
3. What are the differences between human touch and artificial touch?
4. How could AI-powered prosthetic limbs improve the quality of life for people with disabilities?
5. As robots become more common in homes, hospitals, and workplaces, what ethical responsibilities should engineers and society consider when designing machines that physically interact with people?

Key Takeaways

After completing this chapter, you should be able to:

- Explain why AI requires a sense of touch to safely interact with the physical world.
- Describe how tactile, pressure, and force sensors work together.
- Understand how robots use touch sensors to handle delicate objects.
- Identify real-world applications of AI touch sensors in healthcare, manufacturing, agriculture, logistics, and prosthetic technology.
- Explain the purpose of electronic skin (e-skin) and its potential future applications.
- Recognize the differences between human touch and artificial touch.
- Appreciate the importance of safety, ethics, and responsible engineering when developing AI systems that physically interact with humans.

Learn AI. Understand AI. Shape the Future.

— Susie Hala
IntelliGloss Press

Chapter 6

AI's Sense of Motion: Accelerometers, Gyroscopes, and Intelligent Navigation

Imagine trying to walk across a room while keeping your eyes closed and standing on one foot. At first, you might be able to remain balanced for a few seconds, but eventually your body would begin to sway. Without thinking, your muscles would immediately adjust to keep you from falling. Even if you were not looking at the floor, your brain would still know whether you were standing upright, leaning forward, turning your head, or losing your balance. This remarkable ability depends on an incredible system inside your body that constantly measures movement, direction, speed, and balance. Every step you take, every bicycle you ride, and every staircase you climb depends on this hidden navigation system working continuously in the background.

Artificial intelligence faces a similar challenge. Cameras allow AI to observe the environment, microphones allow AI to hear sounds, and tactile sensors help AI interact with physical objects. However, intelligent machines also need to understand how they are moving through space. A self-driving vehicle must know whether it is accelerating, slowing down, turning, or climbing a hill. A drone flying above a forest must constantly maintain its balance while adjusting to wind currents. A humanoid robot walking across a factory floor must know if it is leaning too far forward before it falls. Without the ability to measure movement and orientation, even the most intelligent AI system would quickly lose control of its actions. This challenge led engineers to develop motion sensors that give artificial intelligence an awareness of movement similar to the balance systems found in the human body.

One of the most important motion sensors used in artificial intelligence is the **accelerometer**. An accelerometer measures changes in speed and direction. Whenever an object begins moving, stops moving, speeds up, slows down, or changes direction, the accelerometer detects these changes and converts them into digital information. Although the word "accelerometer" may sound complicated, most people carry one every day without realizing it. Nearly every modern smartphone contains an accelerometer. When you rotate your phone from a vertical position to a horizontal position and the screen automatically changes orientation, the accelerometer is detecting that movement. Fitness watches count your steps by measuring tiny changes in motion. Tablets, gaming controllers, drones, and robots all rely on accelerometers to understand movement.

The accelerometer performs a role similar to part of the human body's balance system. Deep inside each ear is a structure known as the vestibular system. Tiny fluid-filled canals and specialized sensory cells detect movement whenever you walk, jump, turn your head, or ride in a moving vehicle. These signals are immediately sent to your brain, allowing you to maintain balance without consciously thinking about it. Artificial intelligence uses accelerometers in much the same way. The sensor constantly reports changes in motion, allowing computers to adjust movement before problems occur. Although AI does not experience balance in the human sense, accelerometers provide the information necessary for intelligent movement.

Another essential motion sensor is the **gyroscope**. While accelerometers measure changes in speed and direction, gyroscopes measure rotation and orientation. Imagine spinning slowly in a swivel chair. Even with your eyes closed, you know that your body is turning. A gyroscope performs this same task for machines by measuring rotation around different axes. Together, accelerometers and gyroscopes provide AI with a detailed understanding of how an object is moving through three-dimensional space. Modern smartphones combine information from both sensors to improve navigation, gaming, augmented reality, and image stabilization when taking photographs or recording videos.

Understanding the difference between these two sensors is important. Suppose you are riding a bicycle. As you begin pedaling, the accelerometer measures the increase in speed. When you lean into a turn, the gyroscope measures the change in orientation. When you stop at a traffic light, the accelerometer detects that your speed has decreased to zero. Working together, these sensors continuously provide information that describes how movement is changing over time. Artificial intelligence combines these measurements to make decisions about balance, navigation, and control.

In many intelligent systems, accelerometers and gyroscopes are combined into a single device called an **Inertial Measurement Unit**, or **IMU**. An IMU collects information about movement, acceleration, and orientation simultaneously. Engineers use IMUs in aircraft, spacecraft, drones, autonomous vehicles, industrial robots, underwater exploration vehicles, and many other advanced technologies. These systems continue functioning even when GPS signals become weak or unavailable. For example, if a drone briefly loses its satellite connection while flying between tall buildings, its IMU continues measuring movement, helping the AI estimate its current position until GPS becomes available again.

Motion sensing becomes especially important in autonomous vehicles. Imagine a self-driving car traveling along a busy highway. Cameras identify lanes, traffic signs, and nearby vehicles. Radar measures distances to surrounding objects. GPS estimates the vehicle's location on a digital map. Meanwhile, accelerometers and gyroscopes continuously measure speed, steering, braking, and vehicle orientation. Artificial intelligence combines all of this information to maintain safe driving. If the vehicle suddenly encounters a slippery road surface, the motion sensors immediately detect changes in movement that may indicate loss of traction. AI responds by adjusting braking, steering, or acceleration to help maintain control.

Drones provide another excellent example of intelligent motion sensing. Unlike airplanes that generally move forward, drones must constantly maintain balance while hovering in one location. Even a gentle breeze can push a drone away from its intended position. Motion sensors detect these tiny changes almost instantly. AI continuously adjusts the speed of each propeller many times every second to restore stability. Without accelerometers and gyroscopes, drones would become extremely difficult to control and could quickly lose balance during flight.

Humanoid robots depend heavily on motion sensors because walking is much more complicated than it appears. Humans automatically shift body weight from one leg to the other while adjusting muscles to maintain balance. Robots must perform similar calculations electronically. Motion sensors constantly measure body position, foot placement, and center of gravity. Artificial intelligence analyzes this information and calculates how each joint should move to keep the robot standing or walking safely. Every step requires thousands of tiny adjustments that occur almost instantly.

Motion sensing also plays an important role in healthcare. Wearable devices equipped with accelerometers help doctors monitor patient activity, detect falls among elderly individuals, measure rehabilitation progress after surgery, and study movement disorders such as Parkinson's disease. Athletes use motion sensors to improve performance by analyzing running form, jumping technique, and body mechanics. Physical therapists rely on these technologies to measure patient recovery while developing personalized treatment programs. Artificial intelligence transforms these motion measurements into valuable medical insights that help improve patient care.

As artificial intelligence continues advancing, motion sensing technologies are becoming increasingly sophisticated. Researchers are developing robots capable of climbing stairs, navigating rough terrain, exploring disaster zones, assisting astronauts in space, and operating safely alongside humans in workplaces and hospitals. These achievements depend on AI's ability to continuously measure movement while responding intelligently to changing conditions. Every improvement in motion sensing brings intelligent machines one step closer to performing complex physical tasks that require precision, balance, and adaptability.

Motion sensors remind us that intelligence is not simply about solving mathematical problems or recognizing images. True intelligence also involves understanding how to move safely through the physical world. Cameras provide vision. Microphones provide hearing. Tactile sensors provide touch. Accelerometers, gyroscopes, and inertial measurement systems provide movement and balance. Together, these artificial senses allow AI to perceive its surroundings, interact with objects, and navigate environments with increasing confidence and precision. As you continue reading this book, you will discover that combining multiple sensors allows artificial intelligence to build a richer understanding of the world than any single sensor could provide alone.

Learn AI. Understand AI. Shape the Future.

— Susie Hala
IntelliGloss Press

Chapter 6 Summary

Chapter 6 introduced **AI's sense of motion**, explaining how artificial intelligence uses accelerometers, gyroscopes, and inertial measurement units (IMUs) to understand movement, balance, direction, and orientation. Just as humans rely on their inner ear and nervous system to maintain balance and coordinate movement, AI depends on electronic motion sensors to navigate safely through the physical world.

Students learned that an **accelerometer** measures changes in speed and direction, while a **gyroscope** measures rotation and orientation. Together, these sensors allow AI to determine whether a machine is moving, stopping, turning, accelerating, or changing position. By combining information from both sensors, intelligent systems gain a much more complete understanding of how they are moving.

The chapter explained that many modern devices already use motion sensors, including smartphones, smartwatches, gaming controllers, drones, robots, autonomous vehicles, and wearable healthcare devices. These sensors allow AI to perform tasks such as rotating a smartphone screen, stabilizing a drone during flight, maintaining the balance of a humanoid robot, and helping self-driving vehicles safely navigate roads.

Students also learned about **Inertial Measurement Units (IMUs)**, which combine multiple motion sensors into a single system. IMUs are widely used in aircraft, spacecraft, robotics, industrial automation, and autonomous vehicles because they provide continuous movement information even when GPS signals become unavailable.

Finally, the chapter emphasized that AI's ability to move safely depends on combining multiple artificial senses. Vision, hearing, touch, and motion sensing work together to create intelligent systems capable of interacting with complex environments. Understanding motion sensors helps students appreciate how AI continues to become more capable while reminding us that safe and responsible engineering remains essential.

Reflection

Movement is something most people take for granted. We walk, run, ride bicycles, climb stairs, and maintain our balance without consciously thinking about the remarkable biological systems that make these actions possible. Artificial intelligence must solve these same challenges using electronic sensors, mathematics, and machine learning.

Learning about motion sensing demonstrates that intelligence is much more than recognizing images or understanding speech. Intelligent machines must also understand how they move through the physical world while continuously adjusting to changing conditions. As AI-powered robots, vehicles, drones, and wearable devices become more common, engineers must continue improving safety, reliability, and ethical design to ensure these technologies benefit society.

Understanding AI's sense of motion reminds us that every successful intelligent system depends on accurate information collected from multiple sensors working together.

Student Worksheet

Name: ____

Part A – Vocabulary

Define each term using your own words.

1. Accelerometer

2. Gyroscope

3. Inertial Measurement Unit (IMU)

4. Motion Sensor

5. Orientation

Part B – Short Answer

1. Why do intelligent machines need motion sensors?

2. Explain the difference between an accelerometer and a gyroscope.

3. What is an Inertial Measurement Unit (IMU), and why is it useful?

4. List four technologies that depend on motion sensors.

5. Why do autonomous vehicles combine information from multiple sensors?

Part C – Critical Thinking

Imagine you have been hired to help design an AI-powered rescue drone.

Write one paragraph explaining:

- Which motion sensors should the drone use?
- How would those sensors help the drone fly safely?
- What other AI sensors would improve its performance?

Chapter 6 Quiz

Multiple Choice

1. Which sensor measures changes in speed and direction?

A. Camera

B. Accelerometer

C. Microphone

D. Thermometer

2. Which sensor measures rotation and orientation?

A. GPS

B. Gyroscope

C. Radar

D. Pressure Sensor

3. What does IMU stand for?

A. Intelligent Motion Unit

B. Inertial Measurement Unit

C. Internal Mapping Utility

D. Intelligent Mapping Unit

4. Which technology depends heavily on accelerometers and gyroscopes?

A. Self-driving vehicles

B. Paper notebooks

C. Flashlights

D. Calculators

5. Why are motion sensors important for drones?

A. They improve internet speed.

B. They help maintain balance and stable flight.

C. They increase battery size.

D. They store photographs.

True or False

6. _____ Accelerometers measure changes in movement.

7. _____ Gyroscopes measure rotation and orientation.

8. _____ Smartphones commonly contain motion sensors.

9. _____ Motion sensors are important in healthcare.

10. _____ Combining multiple sensors helps AI make better decisions.

Answer Key

Multiple Choice

1. **B** — Accelerometer
2. **B** — Gyroscope
3. **B** — Inertial Measurement Unit
4. **A** — Self-driving vehicles
5. **B** — They help maintain balance and stable flight.

True or False

6. **True**
7. **True**
8. **True**
9. **True**
10. **True**

Bonus Question

Explain why AI should never rely on only one sensor when making important decisions, such as driving a vehicle or flying a drone.

Sample Answer:

Using only one sensor can increase the risk of errors if that sensor becomes blocked, damaged, or provides incorrect information. By combining data from cameras, GPS, accelerometers, gyroscopes, radar, lidar, and other sensors, AI can compare information from multiple sources and make safer, more accurate decisions. This approach improves reliability and reduces the chance of accidents.

Classroom Discussion

1. How is the human balance system similar to the motion sensors used in AI?
2. Why do autonomous vehicles need both accelerometers and gyroscopes?
3. How do motion sensors improve the safety of drones and robots?
4. What are some ways wearable motion sensors can improve healthcare?
5. As AI systems become more mobile, what responsibilities do engineers have to ensure they operate safely around people?

Key Takeaways

After completing this chapter, you should be able to:

- Explain why AI requires motion sensors to move safely through the physical world.
- Describe the functions of accelerometers, gyroscopes, and inertial measurement units (IMUs).
- Understand how AI combines motion sensing with vision, hearing, and touch.
- Identify real-world applications of motion sensors in smartphones, drones, robotics, healthcare, autonomous vehicles, and aerospace.
- Explain why combining multiple sensors improves AI accuracy and safety.
- Recognize the importance of responsible engineering when designing AI systems that move and interact with people.
- Appreciate how motion sensing helps artificial intelligence become more capable, reliable, and adaptable in real-world environments.

Learn AI. Understand AI. Shape the Future.

— Susie Hala
IntelliGloss Press

Chapter 7

AI's Sense of Location: GPS, Mapping, and Geospatial Intelligence

Have you ever opened a navigation app on your smartphone and watched a small blue dot appear exactly where you were standing? Within seconds, the app could tell you which direction you were facing, how many miles remained before reaching your destination, and even estimate the time it would take to arrive. Most people use this technology every day without giving much thought to how it works. It feels almost magical that a device small enough to fit in your pocket can determine your location anywhere on Earth with remarkable accuracy. Behind this everyday convenience lies one of the most extraordinary engineering achievements in human history—a worldwide network of satellites, sensors, computers, and artificial intelligence working together to answer one simple but incredibly important question: **Where am I?**

Knowing your location is one of the most fundamental pieces of information needed to understand the world around you. Imagine trying to give directions to a friend without knowing the names of streets, your current location, or where your destination is located. Even if you could see the buildings around you and hear the sounds of nearby traffic, finding your way would become extremely difficult. Humans constantly rely on location information, often without realizing it. We recognize familiar neighborhoods, remember where we parked our cars, follow maps while traveling, and understand that every place has a relationship to the places surrounding it. Our brains continuously combine visual information, memory, movement, and landmarks to build an internal map of the world.

Artificial intelligence faces a similar challenge. Cameras allow AI to observe objects, microphones allow AI to recognize sounds, tactile sensors allow robots to safely handle physical objects, and motion sensors measure movement and balance. However, none of these sensors alone can answer an important question: **Where is the machine located right now?** A delivery robot must know which sidewalk it is traveling on before delivering a package. A self-driving vehicle must know exactly which lane it occupies before making a turn. A rescue drone searching for missing hikers must understand its precise location so it can report important discoveries to emergency responders. Without accurate location information, intelligent machines would quickly become confused, no matter how advanced their other sensors might be.

One of the most important technologies that gives AI a sense of location is the **Global Positioning System**, more commonly known as **GPS**. GPS is a satellite-based navigation system that allows electronic devices to determine their position almost anywhere on Earth. Many people think GPS is simply an application installed on a smartphone, but GPS is actually a massive technological infrastructure operating high above our planet. Dozens of satellites orbit Earth approximately 12,500 miles (20,200 kilometers) above the surface. These satellites continuously transmit highly accurate timing signals toward Earth twenty-four hours a day. GPS receivers inside smartphones, vehicles, aircraft, ships, drones, tractors, and countless other devices listen to these signals and calculate their location using advanced mathematical formulas.

To better understand GPS, imagine standing in a large open field while four friends stand at different locations around you. If each friend tells you exactly how far away they are, you could eventually determine your own location by comparing those distances. GPS satellites perform a similar task. Each satellite continuously broadcasts its position and the exact time the signal was transmitted. A GPS receiver measures how long it takes each signal to arrive. Because radio waves travel at the speed of light, even tiny differences in travel time allow the receiver to calculate its distance from each satellite. By comparing signals from at least four satellites simultaneously, the receiver can determine its exact location, altitude, and time with extraordinary precision. This mathematical process is called **trilateration**, and it forms the foundation of modern satellite navigation.

Artificial intelligence depends on GPS because intelligent decisions often require accurate location information. Consider a self-driving vehicle traveling through a busy city. Cameras identify pedestrians, bicycles, traffic lights, and road signs. Radar measures distances to nearby vehicles. Motion sensors monitor acceleration and steering. GPS provides another critical piece of information by identifying the vehicle's location on a digital map. AI combines all these sources of information to understand not only what surrounds the vehicle but also where it is within the transportation network. This combination allows the vehicle to determine when to change lanes, prepare for an upcoming turn, or safely exit a highway.

GPS also plays an important role in agriculture, one of the world's oldest industries. Modern farms increasingly use artificial intelligence to improve crop production while reducing waste. GPS-guided tractors can travel across fields with remarkable accuracy, planting seeds in perfectly straight rows while minimizing overlap. Drones equipped with cameras and GPS fly above farmland collecting images that AI analyzes to identify plant diseases, measure crop health, and detect areas requiring additional irrigation or fertilizer. These technologies help farmers produce more food while conserving valuable resources such as water, fuel, and fertilizer.

Emergency response organizations also rely heavily on AI-powered location technologies. During natural disasters such as hurricanes, earthquakes, floods, or wildfires, emergency teams must quickly determine where help is needed most. GPS allows rescue vehicles, helicopters, drones, and emergency personnel to coordinate their movements while artificial intelligence analyzes maps, weather conditions, satellite imagery, and incoming emergency reports. Search-and-rescue drones equipped with cameras, thermal sensors, and GPS can rapidly survey large areas that would otherwise require many hours for human search teams to explore on foot. Every second saved through accurate navigation can make an important difference when lives are at risk.

Location information becomes even more valuable when combined with digital mapping technologies. A map is much more than a picture showing roads and cities. Modern digital maps contain enormous amounts of information about buildings, bridges, rivers, traffic patterns, speed limits, construction zones, hospitals, schools, businesses, hiking trails, and countless other features. Artificial intelligence continuously updates many digital maps using information collected from satellites, survey vehicles, smartphones, drones, and other connected sensors. This process creates living maps that change as the world changes. New roads appear, construction projects begin, traffic conditions shift throughout the day, and AI continuously helps keep mapping information accurate and current.

Another powerful technology closely related to mapping is **Geographic Information Systems**, commonly called **GIS**. GIS combines maps with many different types of information to help people better understand geographic relationships. Imagine looking at a map showing only streets. Now imagine adding layers that display population density, rainfall, elevation, hospitals, schools, wildfire risks, flood zones, transportation routes, wildlife habitats, and weather conditions. Each new layer provides additional knowledge about the same location. Artificial intelligence analyzes these enormous collections of geographic information to identify patterns that would be difficult for humans to recognize on their own. Governments, scientists, businesses, emergency planners, and environmental organizations use GIS every day to make better decisions about communities, natural resources, transportation, and public safety.

As you continue reading this chapter, you will discover that knowing **where** something is becomes even more powerful when artificial intelligence learns **where it should go next**. GPS provides location. Maps provide context. Geospatial intelligence provides understanding. Together, these technologies allow AI to navigate our world with remarkable accuracy while supporting transportation, agriculture, emergency response, scientific research, environmental protection, and countless other applications that improve everyday life.

Learn AI. Understand AI. Shape the Future.

— Susie Hala
IntelliGloss Press

Chapter 7 Summary

Chapter 7 introduced **AI's sense of location**, explaining how artificial intelligence uses the Global Positioning System (GPS), digital maps, and geospatial intelligence to determine where machines are located and how they navigate through the world. Just as humans rely on memory, landmarks, and their sense of direction to find their way, AI depends on satellites, GPS receivers, maps, and advanced algorithms to understand its position and travel safely.

Students learned that the **Global Positioning System (GPS)** is a network of satellites orbiting Earth that continuously transmit signals to GPS receivers. By measuring the time it takes these signals to travel from multiple satellites, AI-powered devices can accurately calculate their location through a mathematical process called **trilateration**. This technology allows smartphones, drones, robots, ships, airplanes, and autonomous vehicles to know where they are almost anywhere on Earth.

The chapter also explored the importance of **digital maps** and **Geographic Information Systems (GIS)**. Unlike traditional paper maps, digital maps are constantly updated with information about roads, traffic, buildings, weather, terrain, and many other geographic features.

AI combines this information with GPS data to make intelligent decisions about navigation, transportation, agriculture, emergency response, and environmental monitoring.

Students discovered that AI uses location information in many industries. Farmers use GPS-guided equipment to improve crop production. Emergency responders use AI mapping systems during natural disasters. Delivery robots navigate sidewalks using digital maps. Self-driving vehicles combine GPS with cameras, radar, and motion sensors to safely travel through complex traffic conditions.

Finally, the chapter emphasized that location alone is not enough. Artificial intelligence becomes far more capable when GPS, maps, cameras, microphones, motion sensors, and touch sensors work together. This combination of technologies allows AI to build a complete understanding of its environment while helping people solve real-world problems more efficiently and safely.

Reflection

Every journey begins by knowing where you are. Humans naturally combine memory, landmarks, and experience to navigate through the world. Artificial intelligence must accomplish the same goal using satellites, GPS receivers, digital maps, and advanced mathematical calculations.

Understanding AI's sense of location reminds us that navigation is much more than moving from one place to another. It involves understanding relationships between locations, choosing safe routes, responding to changing conditions, and making intelligent decisions based on constantly updated information. As AI-powered transportation, robotics, agriculture, and emergency response systems continue advancing, accurate location information will remain one of the most valuable resources available.

Learning how AI navigates the world helps us appreciate the remarkable technologies that quietly support many of the activities we perform every day.

Student Worksheet

Name: ____

Part A – Vocabulary

Define each term using your own words.

1. Global Positioning System (GPS)

---

2. Trilateration

3. Digital Map

4. Geographic Information System (GIS)

5. Geospatial Intelligence

Part B – Short Answer

1. Why does artificial intelligence need to know its location?

2. Explain how GPS satellites help determine location.

3. What is trilateration, and why is it important?

4. Name four industries that depend on GPS and AI navigation.

5. Why are digital maps more useful than traditional paper maps for AI systems?

Part C – Critical Thinking

Imagine you are designing an AI-powered rescue robot to help after an earthquake.

Write one paragraph explaining:

- How GPS would help the robot.
- What other sensors the robot should use.
- How AI could improve search-and-rescue operations.

Chapter 7 Quiz

Multiple Choice

1. What does GPS stand for?

A. Global Positioning System

B. General Processing System

C. Geographic Programming Software

D. Global Protection Service

2. What does GPS primarily help AI determine?

A. Temperature

B. Location

C. Color

D. Sound

3. What mathematical process allows GPS receivers to calculate location?

A. Multiplication

B. Trilateration

C. Division

D. Estimation

4. Which technology combines maps with many different layers of geographic information?

A. Bluetooth

B. Geographic Information System (GIS)

C. Wi-Fi

D. QR Code

5. Which technology commonly combines GPS, cameras, radar, and AI?

A. Flashlight

B. Self-driving vehicle

C. Calculator

D. Television

True or False

6. _____ GPS satellites continuously transmit signals to Earth.

7. _____ AI can use GPS information without digital maps.

8. _____ Geographic Information Systems help analyze geographic data.

9. _____ Farmers use GPS-guided equipment for precision agriculture.

10. _____ AI navigation becomes more accurate when multiple sensors work together.

Answer Key

Multiple Choice

1. **A** — Global Positioning System
2. **B** — Location
3. **B** — Trilateration
4. **B** — Geographic Information System (GIS)
5. **B** — Self-driving vehicle

True or False

6. **True**
7. **False**
8. **True**
9. **True**
10. **True**

Bonus Question

Modern AI navigation systems often combine GPS with cameras, radar, lidar, motion sensors, and digital maps.

Why is using multiple sensors safer than relying on GPS alone?

Sample Answer:

GPS provides location, but it can sometimes become inaccurate because of tall buildings, tunnels, mountains, or interference. By combining GPS with cameras, radar, lidar, motion sensors, and digital maps, AI can compare information from multiple sources, verify its location, avoid obstacles, and make much safer navigation decisions.

Classroom Discussion

1. Why is knowing your location important for both humans and artificial intelligence?
2. How do GPS satellites help AI-powered devices navigate?
3. Why are digital maps constantly updated, and how does AI benefit from these updates?
4. How can GPS and AI improve agriculture, transportation, emergency response, and environmental protection?
5. As AI navigation systems become more advanced, what ethical and safety responsibilities should engineers consider when designing technologies that people depend on every day?

Key Takeaways

After completing this chapter, you should be able to:

- Explain why location is one of the most important pieces of information for artificial intelligence.
- Describe how GPS satellites help AI determine location.
- Understand the basic concept of trilateration.
- Explain the role of digital maps and Geographic Information Systems (GIS).
- Identify real-world applications of AI navigation in transportation, agriculture, robotics, emergency response, and environmental monitoring.
- Understand why AI combines GPS with many other sensors to improve safety and accuracy.
- Appreciate the importance of reliable navigation systems in building intelligent machines that can safely operate in the real world.

Learn AI. Understand AI. Shape the Future.

— Susie Hala
IntelliGloss Press

Chapter 8

Beyond Human Vision: How AI Sees the Invisible World with Lidar, Radar, Infrared, Thermal Imaging, and Hyperspectral Sensors

Imagine standing outside on a beautiful sunny afternoon. You look up and see blue skies filled with white clouds. Trees gently sway in the breeze while birds fly overhead. Cars travel along nearby streets, people walk through parks, and life appears completely normal. Your eyes collect an enormous amount of information about the world around you. They recognize colors, shapes, movement, distance, and familiar faces with remarkable speed. Yet, despite how powerful human vision seems, there is one important fact that surprises many people: **your eyes are actually blind to most of the information that exists around you.**

The human eye can only detect a very small portion of the electromagnetic spectrum known as **visible light**. This narrow band contains the familiar colors of the rainbow—red, orange, yellow, green, blue, indigo, and violet. Everything you have ever seen with your own eyes exists within this tiny slice of the electromagnetic spectrum. However, beyond visible light lies an enormous world of invisible energy. Radio waves carry television broadcasts and wireless internet signals. Microwaves cook food and support satellite communications. Infrared radiation carries heat. Ultraviolet light from the Sun can cause sunburn. X-rays allow doctors to examine broken bones, while gamma rays are produced by some of the most energetic events in the universe. Although these forms of energy surround us every day, our eyes cannot detect them naturally.

Artificial intelligence is not limited by human biology. Engineers have developed specialized sensors capable of detecting many forms of energy that humans cannot see. These technologies allow AI to observe hidden information about the world, creating what could be described as **superhuman perception**. Instead of relying only on ordinary cameras, AI systems may combine lidar, radar, infrared cameras, thermal imaging devices, hyperspectral sensors, ultrasonic sensors, and many other advanced technologies. Each sensor reveals different information about the environment, allowing AI to build a far more complete understanding of the world than human vision alone could provide.

One of the most important technologies in modern artificial intelligence is **lidar**, which stands for **Light Detection and Ranging**. Lidar works by sending millions of invisible laser pulses toward nearby objects every second. These laser pulses bounce off buildings, trees, roads, vehicles, and people before returning to the sensor. By measuring the incredibly small amount of time required for each laser pulse to return, AI calculates the distance to every object with extraordinary precision. The result is a highly detailed three-dimensional map of the surrounding environment.

Imagine entering a completely dark room where you cannot see anything. If you shouted loudly, you would hear your voice echo back from the walls. The amount of time required for the echo to return gives your brain clues about the size of the room. Lidar works using a similar principle, except it uses light instead of sound. Because light travels much faster than sound, lidar can produce highly accurate three-dimensional models within fractions of a second. Autonomous vehicles, construction companies, archaeologists, environmental scientists, and robotic systems all use lidar to understand complex environments with remarkable accuracy.

Another technology that extends AI beyond human vision is **radar**, which stands for **Radio Detection and Ranging**. Unlike lidar, which uses laser light, radar sends radio waves through the environment. These radio waves reflect off objects and return to the radar receiver, allowing AI to calculate distance, direction, and speed. Radar has one important advantage over ordinary cameras: it continues functioning even during heavy rain, dense fog, snowstorms, or complete darkness. This makes radar an essential safety system for self-driving vehicles, commercial aircraft, ships, weather forecasting, and national defense.

Many people experience radar without realizing it. Weather forecasts showing approaching thunderstorms often rely on powerful Doppler radar systems that track rainfall, wind speed, and storm movement across hundreds of miles. Air traffic controllers monitor thousands of aircraft using radar to safely guide flights through crowded skies. Modern vehicles use radar to support adaptive cruise control, automatic emergency braking, and blind-spot monitoring. In each case, AI analyzes radar information to improve safety while helping humans make better decisions.

While radar and lidar measure distance, **infrared sensors** allow AI to detect heat. Every object with a temperature above absolute zero gives off infrared radiation, even though humans cannot naturally see it. Infrared cameras detect this invisible energy and convert it into images that reveal temperature differences across an environment. Firefighters use infrared cameras to locate people trapped inside smoke-filled buildings where ordinary vision becomes impossible. Search-and-rescue teams use thermal cameras to find missing hikers during nighttime operations. Wildlife researchers monitor animal populations without disturbing natural habitats. Doctors study blood circulation and inflammation using medical thermal imaging. During global disease outbreaks, airports have even used thermal cameras to identify travelers with elevated body temperatures.

Artificial intelligence becomes even more powerful when thermal imaging is combined with machine learning. Instead of simply displaying colorful temperature maps, AI analyzes heat patterns to detect abnormalities that might otherwise go unnoticed. Industrial facilities monitor electrical equipment to identify overheating components before failures occur. Utility companies inspect power lines using drones equipped with thermal cameras. Farmers identify irrigation problems by measuring differences in crop temperature. Environmental scientists monitor volcanic activity, wildfires, and changing ocean temperatures from satellites equipped with infrared sensors. Each application demonstrates how AI extends human observation into a world that our eyes alone cannot perceive.

Perhaps one of the most fascinating sensing technologies is **hyperspectral imaging**. Ordinary digital cameras capture three primary colors—red, green, and blue—to create photographs.

Hyperspectral sensors capture hundreds of extremely narrow bands of light across the electromagnetic spectrum. Every material reflects light differently, creating what scientists often describe as a unique spectral fingerprint. Artificial intelligence analyzes these spectral fingerprints to identify materials that appear identical to human eyes.

Imagine looking at two healthy-looking plants growing side by side. To you, both plants may appear equally green and healthy. A hyperspectral camera, however, might detect subtle changes in reflected light that indicate one plant is beginning to suffer from disease several days before visible symptoms appear. Farmers can then treat only the affected areas instead of spraying entire fields, reducing costs while protecting the environment. Similar technologies help scientists locate mineral deposits, monitor water quality, identify pollution, detect illegal mining activities, and study changing ecosystems across the planet.

The true power of artificial intelligence comes not from using a single sensor but from combining many sensors together. Cameras provide visible images. Lidar creates three-dimensional maps. Radar measures movement and performs well during poor weather. Infrared cameras detect heat. Hyperspectral sensors reveal chemical and biological information invisible to human vision. AI combines these multiple sources of information into a unified understanding of the environment. This process, known as **sensor fusion**, allows intelligent systems to make more accurate and reliable decisions than would be possible using any single sensor alone.

As artificial intelligence continues advancing, scientists are developing even more sophisticated sensing technologies capable of exploring deep oceans, distant planets, microscopic biological structures, and complex environmental systems. Future AI may detect changes that humans have never been able to observe directly, leading to breakthroughs in medicine, climate science, astronomy, engineering, agriculture, and many other fields. These remarkable technologies remind us that artificial intelligence is not replacing human vision—it is expanding it, allowing humanity to explore an invisible world that has always existed but remained beyond the limits of our natural senses.

Learn AI. Understand AI. Shape the Future.

— Susie Hala
IntelliGloss Press

Chapter 8 Summary

Chapter 8 explored how artificial intelligence can detect information that is invisible to the human eye by using advanced sensing technologies such as **lidar, radar, infrared sensors, thermal imaging, and hyperspectral imaging**. While humans can only see visible light, AI can analyze many different forms of energy across the electromagnetic spectrum, allowing intelligent systems to observe the world in ways that people cannot naturally experience.

Students learned that human vision is limited to the visible portion of the electromagnetic spectrum. Artificial intelligence overcomes this limitation by using specialized sensors that collect information from invisible forms of energy. These sensors provide AI with additional data that improves decision-making, navigation, scientific research, healthcare, agriculture, environmental monitoring, and many other applications.

The chapter explained how **lidar** uses laser pulses to create highly accurate three-dimensional maps of the surrounding environment. Students discovered that lidar is widely used in autonomous vehicles, robotics, archaeology, construction, and environmental mapping because it measures distances with remarkable precision.

The chapter also introduced **radar**, which uses radio waves instead of light. Radar allows AI to detect objects even during heavy rain, fog, snow, or complete darkness. Students learned how radar supports weather forecasting, aviation, shipping, national defense, and driver-assistance systems in modern vehicles.

Students explored **infrared and thermal imaging**, learning that every object above absolute zero emits heat energy. Infrared sensors detect this invisible heat, allowing firefighters to locate people through smoke, doctors to identify medical conditions, utility companies to inspect electrical equipment, and environmental scientists to monitor wildfires and changing ecosystems.

Finally, students learned about **hyperspectral imaging**, one of the most advanced sensing technologies available today. Unlike ordinary cameras that capture only red, green, and blue light, hyperspectral sensors collect hundreds of narrow wavelengths, creating detailed "spectral fingerprints" that help AI identify materials, monitor crops, detect pollution, discover minerals, and study environmental changes.

The chapter concluded by explaining that AI becomes most powerful when it combines information from many different sensors through **sensor fusion**, allowing intelligent systems to understand the world more accurately than any single sensor could achieve alone.

Reflection

Human vision is one of our greatest strengths, yet it represents only a tiny fraction of the information surrounding us. Artificial intelligence demonstrates that the world contains much more than what our eyes can naturally observe. By using lidar, radar, infrared cameras, thermal imaging, and hyperspectral sensors, AI helps humanity explore hidden information that supports scientific discovery, improves safety, protects the environment, and advances healthcare.

Understanding these technologies reminds us that artificial intelligence is not replacing human abilities—it is expanding them. AI gives people new ways to observe and understand complex systems that would otherwise remain invisible. As these sensing technologies continue advancing, they will create exciting opportunities while also requiring responsible decision-making to ensure they are used ethically, safely, and for the benefit of society.

Student Worksheet

Name: ______________________________

Part A – Vocabulary

Define each term using your own words.

1. Electromagnetic Spectrum

____

____

2. Lidar

____

____

3. Radar

____

____

4. Thermal Imaging

____

____

5. Hyperspectral Imaging

____

____

____

Part B – Short Answer

1. Why can artificial intelligence detect things that humans cannot naturally see?

____

____

____

2. Explain how lidar creates a three-dimensional map.

3. Why is radar useful during bad weather?

4. How does thermal imaging help firefighters and emergency responders?

5. What is the advantage of combining multiple sensors through sensor fusion?

Part C – Critical Thinking

Imagine you are leading a scientific expedition to study a rainforest.

Write one paragraph explaining:

- Which AI sensing technologies would you use?
- What information would each sensor collect?
- How could AI help scientists better understand and protect the rainforest?

Chapter 8 Quiz

Multiple Choice

1. Which part of the electromagnetic spectrum can humans naturally see?

A. Infrared

B. Visible Light

C. Radio Waves

D. X-rays

2. Which technology uses laser pulses to measure distance?

A. Radar

B. GPS

C. Lidar

D. Sonar

3. Which technology uses radio waves to detect objects?

A. Thermal Imaging

B. Radar

C. Camera

D. GPS

4. What type of energy does an infrared camera detect?

A. Sound

B. Heat

C. Electricity

D. Gravity

5. What makes hyperspectral imaging different from a regular digital camera?

A. It captures only black-and-white images.

B. It records hundreds of wavelengths of light instead of only red, green, and blue.

C. It cannot be used outdoors.

D. It only works underwater.

True or False

6. _____ Human eyes can naturally see infrared radiation.

7. _____ Lidar helps autonomous vehicles understand their surroundings.

8. _____ Radar can operate during heavy fog and rain.

9. _____ Thermal imaging detects heat differences.

10. _____ Sensor fusion combines information from multiple sensors to improve AI decision-making.

Answer Key

Multiple Choice

1. **B** — Visible Light
2. **C** — Lidar
3. **B** — Radar
4. **B** — Heat
5. **B** — It records hundreds of wavelengths of light instead of only red, green, and blue.

True or False

6. **False**
7. **True**
8. **True**
9. **True**
10. **True**

Bonus Question

Artificial intelligence often combines cameras, lidar, radar, thermal imaging, GPS, and other sensors into a single intelligent system.

Why is this combination more effective than relying on only one sensor?

Sample Answer:

Each sensor collects different types of information and has different strengths and limitations. Cameras provide detailed visual images, lidar measures precise distances, radar works well in poor weather, thermal cameras detect heat, and GPS provides location. When AI combines all of these data sources through sensor fusion, it creates a more complete and reliable understanding of the environment, leading to safer and more accurate decisions.

Classroom Discussion

1. Why can AI detect information that humans cannot naturally see?
2. How do lidar and radar differ, and why are both important?
3. How is thermal imaging used in healthcare, firefighting, and environmental science?
4. What are some advantages of hyperspectral imaging in agriculture and environmental monitoring?
5. As AI gains the ability to observe more of the invisible world, what ethical responsibilities should scientists, engineers, and governments consider?

Key Takeaways

After completing this chapter, you should be able to:

- Explain why human vision is limited to visible light.
- Describe how lidar, radar, infrared, thermal imaging, and hyperspectral sensors extend AI's perception.
- Understand the basic principles behind each sensing technology.

- Identify real-world applications of these advanced sensors in transportation, healthcare, agriculture, environmental science, robotics, and public safety.
- Explain the concept of sensor fusion and why combining multiple sensors improves AI performance.
- Recognize the importance of using advanced sensing technologies responsibly and ethically.
- Appreciate how artificial intelligence expands humanity's ability to observe, understand, and solve complex real-world challenges.

Learn AI. Understand AI. Shape the Future.

— Susie Hala
IntelliGloss Press

Chapter 9

AI Above the Earth: How Satellites Help Artificial Intelligence Observe Our Planet

Have you ever looked up at the night sky and wondered what is happening hundreds of miles above your head? Most people see stars, the Moon, and perhaps an airplane crossing the darkness. What many people do not realize is that thousands of satellites are also traveling silently around our planet every day. These satellites are not simply floating through space. They are constantly collecting information about Earth, taking photographs, measuring temperatures, tracking storms, monitoring forests, observing oceans, detecting pollution, guiding airplanes and ships, supporting communication networks, and helping people navigate almost anywhere in the world. Together, these orbiting machines provide one of the most important sources of information used by modern artificial intelligence.

Throughout this book, you have learned that AI depends on sensors to understand the world. Cameras allow AI to see. Microphones allow AI to hear. Tactile sensors allow AI to detect touch. Motion sensors measure movement, while GPS provides location. In the previous chapter, you discovered that lidar, radar, infrared, and hyperspectral sensors allow AI to observe information beyond normal human vision. In this chapter, those same sensing technologies move into space. Satellites become giant observation platforms that continuously gather information about our planet from hundreds of miles above the Earth's surface. Artificial intelligence analyzes this enormous stream of information to help scientists, governments, businesses, farmers, engineers, and emergency responders make better decisions.

A satellite is an object that travels in orbit around another object. The Moon is Earth's natural satellite because it circles our planet through the force of gravity. Artificial satellites are different because they are built by people and launched into space using powerful rockets. Once in orbit, satellites travel at incredible speeds while remaining high above Earth's atmosphere. Depending on their mission, satellites may orbit only a few hundred miles above Earth or tens of thousands of miles into space. Some satellites circle the Earth every ninety minutes, while others remain positioned above the same location, continuously observing a particular region.

Artificial intelligence depends on satellites because they provide something no ground-based sensor can offer—a global view. Imagine standing in the middle of a large forest. You can observe the trees immediately surrounding you, but you cannot see the entire forest at once. A satellite, however, can photograph thousands of square miles during a single pass over Earth. By combining images collected over days, weeks, months, and years, AI can identify patterns that would be impossible for humans to detect from ground level. Scientists use these observations to monitor deforestation, shrinking glaciers, changing coastlines, expanding cities, crop growth, ocean temperatures, air pollution, and countless other environmental changes occurring across the planet.

Modern satellites carry many different types of sensors, each designed to collect specific kinds of information. Some satellites contain extremely powerful digital cameras capable of capturing images detailed enough to identify roads, buildings, bridges, rivers, and agricultural fields. Others use infrared sensors to measure heat emitted from forests, oceans, volcanoes, and cities. Radar satellites can observe Earth's surface through clouds, smoke, and darkness by sending radio waves toward the planet and measuring the reflected signals. Hyperspectral satellites collect hundreds of wavelengths of light that allow AI to identify minerals, vegetation, water quality, and even subtle chemical changes invisible to ordinary cameras. Every satellite contributes another piece to the enormous puzzle that artificial intelligence assembles into a detailed understanding of our planet.

One of the most valuable applications of satellite imagery is **weather forecasting**. Every day, meteorologists depend on satellites to observe clouds forming over oceans, monitor hurricanes developing in tropical regions, track thunderstorms crossing continents, and measure changes in atmospheric conditions. Artificial intelligence analyzes millions of satellite observations collected every hour to improve weather prediction models. By recognizing patterns hidden within enormous amounts of historical weather data, AI helps forecasters predict storms more accurately and earlier than ever before. These predictions allow communities to prepare for hurricanes, floods, blizzards, tornadoes, and other dangerous weather events, helping save lives and reduce property damage.

Satellites also play a critical role in protecting Earth's environment. Forests, wetlands, rivers, lakes, coral reefs, glaciers, and oceans are constantly changing due to both natural processes and human activity. Artificial intelligence compares satellite images collected over many years to detect gradual changes that may be difficult for people to notice. AI can identify illegal logging in remote forests, monitor melting polar ice, measure drought conditions affecting farmland, detect harmful algae blooms in lakes, and track the spread of wildfires across large landscapes. Environmental scientists use these observations to better understand climate change while developing strategies to protect ecosystems for future generations.

Agriculture has also been transformed by satellite technology and artificial intelligence. Farmers no longer rely solely on walking through fields to evaluate crop conditions. Satellites continuously photograph farmland throughout the growing season while AI analyzes these images to identify areas experiencing water shortages, insect damage, nutrient deficiencies, or plant diseases. Instead of treating entire fields equally, farmers can apply water, fertilizer, or pesticides only where needed. This approach, known as **precision agriculture**, helps increase crop production while reducing costs, conserving natural resources, and protecting the environment.

Disaster response organizations also depend heavily on satellite observations. After hurricanes, earthquakes, floods, volcanic eruptions, or major wildfires, emergency responders must quickly understand the extent of damage across large areas. Satellites can photograph affected regions within hours while artificial intelligence compares new images with photographs taken before the disaster occurred. AI identifies damaged buildings, blocked roads, flooded neighborhoods, collapsed bridges, and isolated communities requiring immediate assistance. Rescue teams then use this information to prioritize resources where they are needed most, often saving valuable time during life-threatening emergencies.

Satellites demonstrate one of the most remarkable strengths of artificial intelligence. AI does not become intelligent simply because it contains powerful algorithms. It becomes intelligent because it receives information from many different sources. Cameras on the ground show what is happening at street level. Sensors inside vehicles monitor movement. GPS provides location. Satellites reveal the broader picture from space. By combining all of these perspectives, artificial intelligence develops a far richer understanding of the world than any single sensor could provide on its own.

As you continue reading this chapter, you will discover that satellites do much more than take pictures of Earth. They help guide ships across oceans, support aircraft navigation, provide internet connections to remote communities, monitor climate change, assist scientific research, and even explore distant planets throughout our solar system. Artificial intelligence transforms the enormous amount of information collected by these orbiting laboratories into knowledge that benefits nearly every aspect of modern society. The partnership between satellites and AI is helping humanity observe our world in ways that were once considered impossible.

Learn AI. Understand AI. Shape the Future.

— **Susie Hala**
IntelliGloss Press

Chapter 9 Summary

Chapter 9 explored how **satellites and artificial intelligence work together** to observe, monitor, and better understand our planet. Students learned that satellites orbit Earth while continuously collecting enormous amounts of information about land, oceans, weather, forests, cities, agriculture, and the atmosphere. Artificial intelligence analyzes this information to recognize patterns, solve problems, and support decision-making across many industries.

The chapter explained that satellites are much more than cameras in space. They carry a wide variety of advanced sensors, including digital cameras, infrared sensors, radar systems, and hyperspectral imaging devices. Each sensor collects different types of information that AI combines to create a more complete understanding of Earth.

Students discovered that AI uses satellite data to improve weather forecasting by tracking storms, hurricanes, cloud formations, and atmospheric conditions. AI also helps scientists monitor climate change by studying glaciers, forests, oceans, rising sea levels, and environmental changes occurring over long periods of time.

The chapter also introduced the concept of **precision agriculture**, where farmers use satellite imagery and artificial intelligence to monitor crop health, detect disease, improve irrigation, and increase food production while conserving natural resources. Emergency responders also depend on satellites and AI to quickly assess damage caused by hurricanes, floods, earthquakes, wildfires, and other natural disasters.

Finally, the chapter emphasized that satellites provide AI with a global perspective that ground-based sensors cannot achieve. When satellite observations are combined with cameras, GPS, motion sensors, weather stations, and many other technologies, artificial intelligence develops a much broader understanding of the world. This ability allows AI to support scientific research, environmental protection, transportation, agriculture, disaster response, and many other fields that improve life on Earth.

Reflection

Looking at Earth from space changes our perspective. Instead of seeing only one street, one neighborhood, or one city, satellites allow humanity to observe entire continents, oceans, weather systems, and ecosystems at the same time. Artificial intelligence transforms these enormous collections of images and measurements into valuable knowledge that helps people make better decisions.

Understanding satellite technology reminds us that many of today's most important scientific discoveries depend on observing patterns over large areas and long periods of time. Artificial intelligence helps humans recognize these patterns more quickly and accurately than ever before.

As satellite technology continues advancing, society must ensure that these powerful observation systems are used responsibly, ethically, and for the benefit of humanity while protecting privacy, national security, and the environment.

Student Worksheet

Name: ______________________________________

Part A – Vocabulary

Define each vocabulary word using your own words.

1. Satellite

____
____

2. Orbit

____
____

3. Earth Observation

____
____

4. Precision Agriculture

____
____

5. Climate Monitoring

____
____
____

Part B – Short Answer

1. Why are satellites important to artificial intelligence?

____
____
____

2. Name four types of sensors commonly found on satellites.

3. How does AI improve weather forecasting?

4. Explain how satellite imagery helps farmers.

5. Why are satellites valuable during natural disasters?

Part C – Critical Thinking

Imagine you are leading a team of scientists studying climate change.

Write one paragraph explaining:

- What information satellites should collect.
- How artificial intelligence would analyze the data.
- How your discoveries could help protect the environment.

Chapter 9 Quiz

Multiple Choice

1. What is the primary purpose of Earth observation satellites?

A. To create music

B. To collect information about Earth from space

C. To repair automobiles

D. To build roads

2. Which technology helps AI monitor hurricanes and storms?

A. Satellites

B. Flashlights

C. Calculators

D. Elevators

3. What is precision agriculture?

A. Building tractors

B. Using satellite data and AI to improve farming

C. Designing airplanes

D. Creating video games

4. Which environmental change can AI monitor using satellite images?

A. Forest loss

B. Glacier melting

C. Ocean temperatures

D. All of the above

5. Why are satellites valuable during disasters?

A. They provide updated images that help emergency responders assess damage.

B. They replace firefighters.

C. They eliminate severe weather.

D. They repair damaged buildings.

True or False

6. _____ Satellites continuously collect information while orbiting Earth.

7. _____ AI analyzes satellite data to identify patterns.

8. _____ Satellites help improve weather forecasting.

9. _____ Farmers can use satellite imagery to improve crop management.

10. _____ Satellite observations can support disaster response and environmental protection.

Answer Key

Multiple Choice

1. **B** — To collect information about Earth from space
2. **A** — Satellites
3. **B** — Using satellite data and AI to improve farming
4. **D** — All of the above
5. **A** — They provide updated images that help emergency responders assess damage.

True or False

6. **True**
7. **True**
8. **True**
9. **True**
10. **True**

Bonus Question

Artificial intelligence often combines information from satellites with GPS, drones, weather stations, cameras, and many other sensors.

Why does combining these different sources of information produce better results than relying on satellites alone?

Sample Answer:

Each sensor collects different kinds of information. Satellites provide a global view, GPS identifies location, drones capture close-up images, weather stations measure local conditions, and cameras observe activity on the ground. Artificial intelligence combines all of these data sources through sensor fusion to build a more complete, accurate, and reliable understanding of the environment, allowing better decisions to be made.

Classroom Discussion

1. Why do satellites give AI an advantage that ground-based sensors cannot provide?
2. How does AI help scientists better understand climate change?
3. In what ways does satellite technology improve agriculture and food production?
4. How can satellite observations help communities prepare for hurricanes, floods, and wildfires?
5. As satellite technology becomes more powerful, how should governments and scientists balance scientific discovery, environmental protection, national security, and individual privacy?

Key Takeaways

After completing this chapter, you should be able to:

- Explain how satellites collect information about Earth.
- Describe the role of artificial intelligence in analyzing satellite data.
- Identify different types of satellite sensors and the information they collect.

- Understand how AI improves weather forecasting, agriculture, environmental monitoring, and disaster response.
- Explain why satellites provide a global perspective that ground-based sensors cannot.
- Recognize the importance of combining satellite observations with other AI sensors.
- Appreciate the role of satellites and artificial intelligence in helping humanity better understand and protect our planet.

Learn AI. Understand AI. Shape the Future.

— Susie Hala
IntelliGloss Press

Chapter 10

Connecting the World: Smart Homes, Smart Cities, and the Internet of Things

Imagine waking up in a home that quietly prepares for your day before you even get out of bed. The thermostat has already adjusted the temperature to a comfortable level. The coffee maker begins brewing your favorite drink at the same time every morning. Window shades slowly open as the Sun rises, allowing natural light to enter the room. Your smart watch has already monitored your sleep, measured your heart rate, and recorded your activity during the night. As you leave for school or work, the lights automatically turn off, the doors lock themselves, and the security system activates without anyone touching a switch. Throughout the day, your home continues monitoring energy use, detecting unusual activity, and adjusting systems to improve comfort, safety, and efficiency. What once seemed like science fiction is becoming an everyday reality because of artificial intelligence and a rapidly growing network of connected devices.

Throughout this book, you have learned that artificial intelligence depends on sensors to understand the world. Cameras provide vision. Microphones collect sound. Touch sensors measure pressure. Motion sensors detect movement. GPS provides location. Lidar, radar, and thermal sensors reveal information beyond human sight. Satellites observe Earth from space. Individually, each sensor provides valuable information. However, artificial intelligence becomes even more powerful when these sensors communicate with one another through connected networks. This worldwide network of connected devices is known as the **Internet of Things**, often shortened to **IoT**.

The Internet of Things refers to billions of physical devices connected to the internet that continuously collect, share, and exchange information. These devices include smartphones, televisions, thermostats, security cameras, refrigerators, automobiles, factory machines, traffic lights, medical equipment, farm machinery, weather stations, and countless other technologies.

Unlike traditional computers that wait for people to enter information, IoT devices constantly gather data from the environment using built-in sensors. Artificial intelligence analyzes this information, identifies patterns, and often makes decisions automatically without requiring direct human involvement.

To understand the Internet of Things more clearly, imagine the human body. Your eyes constantly collect visual information. Your ears detect sound. Your skin senses temperature and pressure. Your inner ear helps maintain balance. Your brain receives information from every part of your body, combines these signals, and decides how to respond. The Internet of Things works in a similar way. Instead of nerve cells connecting organs to the brain, communication networks connect billions of sensors to artificial intelligence systems. Each sensor contributes one small piece of information. AI combines these pieces into a much larger understanding of homes, businesses, cities, transportation systems, hospitals, and industries. This process allows intelligent systems to respond more quickly and efficiently than would be possible using isolated devices.

One of the easiest places to observe the Internet of Things is inside a modern smart home. A smart home contains devices capable of communicating with one another while sharing information through wireless networks. Motion sensors may detect when someone enters a room and automatically turn on the lights. Smart thermostats monitor indoor temperatures while learning the family's daily routines to reduce energy use. Water leak sensors alert homeowners before small plumbing problems become expensive repairs. Smoke detectors communicate with smartphones, allowing homeowners to receive emergency alerts even when they are away from home. Smart doorbells equipped with cameras allow residents to see visitors from anywhere in the world using mobile applications. Artificial intelligence coordinates these individual systems, helping homes become safer, more comfortable, and more energy efficient.

Energy conservation provides an excellent example of how AI improves everyday life through smart homes. Imagine leaving your house on a hot summer afternoon while accidentally forgetting to adjust the air conditioner. Traditional heating and cooling systems would continue operating even though no one remained inside the house. A smart home uses motion sensors, occupancy detectors, smartphones, and artificial intelligence to recognize that the home is empty. AI automatically adjusts the thermostat, reducing energy consumption while lowering electricity costs. When family members begin traveling home, GPS information from their smartphones may allow the AI system to restore comfortable temperatures before they arrive. This continuous adjustment improves efficiency while reducing unnecessary energy use.

Healthcare is another area where connected devices are transforming daily life. Wearable fitness trackers monitor heart rate, sleep quality, physical activity, and blood oxygen levels throughout the day. Some medical devices continuously measure blood glucose for individuals living with diabetes. Smart medication dispensers remind patients when it is time to take prescriptions. Emergency alert devices automatically contact caregivers if a fall is detected. Artificial intelligence analyzes this information to identify trends that may help physicians detect health problems earlier than traditional medical examinations alone. Rather than replacing doctors, these connected technologies provide additional information that supports better medical decision-making.

The same ideas that improve individual homes can also improve entire communities. A **smart city** uses connected sensors, communication networks, and artificial intelligence to improve public services, transportation, energy use, environmental protection, and public safety. Instead of managing each city department independently, smart cities allow information to flow between transportation systems, emergency services, utilities, environmental monitoring stations, and government agencies. AI analyzes this information to identify opportunities for improving efficiency while reducing costs and improving quality of life for residents.

Traffic management provides one of the clearest examples of how smart cities operate. Traditional traffic lights often follow fixed schedules regardless of how many vehicles are actually waiting at an intersection. Smart traffic systems use cameras, motion sensors, radar, and artificial intelligence to monitor traffic flow continuously. When congestion begins developing, AI adjusts traffic signal timing to improve vehicle movement. Emergency vehicles may receive priority by automatically changing traffic lights along their route. Public transportation systems can adjust schedules based on changing passenger demand. These improvements reduce travel times, decrease fuel consumption, and lower air pollution caused by unnecessary traffic congestion.

Artificial intelligence also helps cities monitor environmental conditions. Air quality sensors continuously measure pollution levels across different neighborhoods. Weather stations monitor temperature, rainfall, humidity, and wind conditions. Water quality sensors observe rivers, lakes, and drinking water systems. Noise sensors identify areas experiencing excessive sound pollution. AI analyzes information collected from these sensors to help city leaders make informed decisions about environmental protection, public health, and urban planning. Instead of waiting for problems to become severe, cities can respond more quickly because intelligent systems provide continuous monitoring.

As you continue reading this chapter, you will discover that smart homes and smart cities represent only the beginning of the Internet of Things. Factories, hospitals, farms, transportation systems, power grids, and even entire countries are becoming increasingly connected through billions of intelligent devices. Artificial intelligence serves as the "brain" that analyzes information collected by these devices, helping people solve problems more efficiently while creating opportunities that previous generations could scarcely imagine.

Learn AI. Understand AI. Shape the Future.

— Susie Hala
IntelliGloss Press

Chapter 10 Summary

Chapter 10 introduced the **Internet of Things (IoT)** and explained how artificial intelligence connects billions of smart devices to create intelligent homes, cities, businesses, and communities. Students learned that while individual sensors collect valuable information, AI becomes much more powerful when those sensors communicate and share data through connected networks.

The chapter explained that the Internet of Things consists of everyday devices equipped with sensors and internet connections. These devices include smartphones, smart thermostats, security cameras, appliances, wearable fitness trackers, traffic lights, medical equipment, factory machines, and agricultural technologies. AI continuously analyzes the information collected by these devices to recognize patterns, improve efficiency, and automate many routine tasks.

Students explored how **smart homes** use AI to improve comfort, safety, and energy efficiency. Motion sensors automatically turn lights on and off, smart thermostats learn household routines to reduce energy consumption, security cameras monitor property, and water leak sensors detect plumbing problems before they become serious. Artificial intelligence coordinates these devices to create homes that respond intelligently to changing conditions.

The chapter also introduced the concept of **smart cities**, where thousands of connected sensors help improve transportation, public safety, environmental monitoring, and city services. AI analyzes information collected from traffic cameras, weather stations, pollution monitors, and public transportation systems to reduce traffic congestion, improve emergency response, conserve energy, and enhance the quality of life for residents.

Finally, students learned that the Internet of Things is expanding into healthcare, agriculture, manufacturing, education, transportation, and many other industries. As billions of connected devices continue generating enormous amounts of information, artificial intelligence will play an increasingly important role in helping people make smarter decisions while creating safer, healthier, and more efficient communities.

Reflection

The Internet of Things demonstrates that artificial intelligence is no longer limited to computers or smartphones. AI is becoming part of the physical world through billions of connected devices that continuously collect, share, and analyze information. Every smart thermostat, wearable fitness tracker, traffic sensor, and connected appliance contributes to a growing network that helps people solve everyday problems.

As these technologies become more common, understanding how connected systems operate becomes increasingly important. While AI and IoT offer tremendous opportunities to improve healthcare, transportation, energy conservation, and public safety, they also require careful attention to privacy, cybersecurity, and responsible technology use. Intelligent systems should always be designed to improve people's lives while protecting their personal information and maintaining public trust.

Learning about the Internet of Things helps us understand that the future of artificial intelligence is not just about smarter computers—it is about creating smarter environments where technology works together to support people in meaningful ways.

Student Worksheet

Name: ____

Part A – Vocabulary

Define each term using your own words.

1. Internet of Things (IoT)

____

____

2. Smart Home

____

____

3. Smart City

____

____

4. Connected Device

____

____

5. Automation

____

____

____

Part B – Short Answer

1. What is the Internet of Things (IoT)?

____

2. Explain how AI helps smart homes become more efficient.

3. Give four examples of IoT devices that people use every day.

4. How does AI improve traffic management in smart cities?

5. Why are connected sensors valuable for healthcare and environmental monitoring?

Part C – Critical Thinking

Imagine your city plans to become a smart city over the next ten years.

Write one paragraph explaining:

- Which smart technologies you would install first.
- How artificial intelligence would improve daily life.
- What privacy and cybersecurity protections should be included.

Chapter 10 Quiz

Multiple Choice

1. What does IoT stand for?

A. Internet of Things

B. Intelligent Online Technology

C. Integrated Operating Terminal

D. Information of Technology

2. What is the primary purpose of the Internet of Things?

A. To print documents

B. To connect devices so they can collect and share information

C. To replace electricity

D. To create websites

3. Which of the following is an example of a smart home device?

A. Smart thermostat

B. Paper calendar

C. Flashlight

D. Notebook

4. How can AI improve traffic in a smart city?

A. By changing traffic signal timing based on real-time traffic conditions

B. By removing all traffic lights

C. By closing roads permanently

D. By increasing speed limits everywhere

5. Which statement best describes artificial intelligence in the Internet of Things?

A. AI analyzes information collected by connected devices to help make better decisions.

B. AI only works on desktop computers.

C. AI can function without collecting information.

D. AI replaces all human decision-making.

True or False

6. _____ Smart homes use connected sensors and AI to improve comfort and safety.

7. _____ Smart cities can use AI to improve transportation and environmental monitoring.

8. _____ IoT devices do not collect information.

9. _____ Healthcare can benefit from wearable IoT devices.

10. _____ Privacy and cybersecurity are important considerations when using connected devices.

Answer Key

Multiple Choice

1. **A** — Internet of Things
2. **B** — To connect devices so they can collect and share information
3. **A** — Smart thermostat
4. **A** — By changing traffic signal timing based on real-time traffic conditions

5. **A** — AI analyzes information collected by connected devices to help make better decisions.

True or False

6. **True**
7. **True**
8. **False**
9. **True**
10. **True**

Bonus Question

Imagine that billions of IoT devices are connected throughout a city.

Why is cybersecurity just as important as artificial intelligence when designing these systems?

Sample Answer:

Cybersecurity protects connected devices and the information they collect from hackers, unauthorized access, and cyberattacks. Without strong cybersecurity, AI systems could receive false information, make incorrect decisions, or expose sensitive personal data. Protecting connected systems helps ensure that AI remains safe, reliable, and trustworthy.

Classroom Discussion

1. How does the Internet of Things make artificial intelligence more powerful?
2. What are some advantages and challenges of living in a smart home?
3. How can smart cities improve transportation, public safety, and environmental protection?
4. Why is cybersecurity essential for billions of connected IoT devices?
5. As AI and IoT continue expanding, how can governments, businesses, engineers, and citizens work together to protect privacy while encouraging innovation?

Key Takeaways

After completing this chapter, you should be able to:

- Explain what the Internet of Things (IoT) is and how it works.
- Describe how AI connects and analyzes information from billions of smart devices.
- Identify examples of smart home and smart city technologies.
- Understand how IoT improves healthcare, transportation, agriculture, manufacturing, and environmental monitoring.
- Explain the importance of connected sensors in modern AI systems.
- Recognize the need for privacy, cybersecurity, and responsible technology development.
- Appreciate how AI and the Internet of Things are transforming everyday life and shaping the intelligent communities of the future.

Learn AI. Understand AI. Shape the Future.

— Susie Hala
IntelliGloss Press

Chapter 11

Sensor Fusion: How Artificial Intelligence Combines Information to Make Intelligent Decisions

Imagine trying to solve a puzzle while only looking at one piece at a time. Each piece contains a small amount of information, but by itself it tells you very little. One piece might show part of a blue sky, another a green tree, and another a person's hand. Until all of the pieces are connected, it is difficult to understand the complete picture. The human brain works in much the same way. Every second, your eyes, ears, skin, muscles, and inner ear collect different kinds of information about the world around you. Your brain combines these separate pieces into one complete understanding of your surroundings. This remarkable ability allows you to recognize people, avoid danger, maintain balance, and make decisions almost instantly.

Artificial intelligence faces the same challenge. Cameras provide images. Microphones collect sounds. Motion sensors detect movement. GPS identifies location. Pressure sensors measure physical contact. Thermal cameras detect heat. Radar measures speed and distance. Lidar creates three-dimensional maps. Individually, each sensor provides valuable information, but none of them tells the complete story. A camera may recognize a pedestrian crossing the street, but it cannot accurately measure the person's speed in poor weather. Radar can measure speed but cannot identify facial expressions. GPS provides location but cannot detect obstacles directly in front of a vehicle. Artificial intelligence becomes much more reliable when it combines information from all of these sensors into one unified understanding of the environment. This process is called **sensor fusion**.

Sensor fusion is one of the most important technologies in modern artificial intelligence because it allows machines to make better decisions using multiple sources of information instead of relying on only one. Rather than trusting a single sensor, AI compares information from many sensors simultaneously. If one sensor provides incomplete or incorrect information, the other sensors help verify what is actually happening. This approach greatly improves accuracy, reliability, and safety while reducing the chances of making poor decisions based on limited data.

A self-driving vehicle provides one of the clearest examples of sensor fusion in action. Imagine an autonomous vehicle approaching a busy intersection on a rainy afternoon. Water droplets on the windshield reduce camera visibility. Bright reflections from wet pavement make it more difficult to recognize lane markings. Fortunately, the vehicle is not relying only on cameras. Radar continues measuring the distance and speed of nearby vehicles despite the rain. Lidar produces a detailed three-dimensional map of the intersection. GPS identifies the vehicle's location on a digital map, while motion sensors monitor steering, acceleration, and braking. Artificial intelligence combines all of this information to create a highly accurate understanding of the environment before deciding whether it is safe to continue through the intersection. If one sensor becomes temporarily less reliable, the remaining sensors continue providing valuable information.

Human beings naturally perform sensor fusion every day without realizing it. Imagine walking through your home late at night after the lights have been turned off. Your eyes provide very little information because the room is dark. Instead, your ears help you recognize familiar sounds, your feet detect the floor beneath you, your hands feel nearby walls, and your memory helps you remember where furniture is located. Your brain automatically combines these different sources of information, allowing you to move safely even with limited visibility. Artificial intelligence uses sensor fusion for the same reason. Combining multiple sources of information creates a much more dependable understanding of the world than relying on any single sensor.

Healthcare is another field where sensor fusion is improving patient care. Modern hospitals use many different monitoring devices to observe patients. Heart monitors measure heart rhythm. Blood pressure monitors track circulation. Pulse oximeters measure blood oxygen levels. Temperature sensors detect fever. Medical imaging devices such as X-rays, CT scans, MRI scanners, and ultrasound systems provide detailed views inside the human body. Artificial intelligence combines information from these different sources to help physicians identify patterns that may indicate illness, injury, or changes in a patient's condition. Rather than depending on one measurement alone, AI evaluates multiple pieces of evidence before supporting clinical decision-making.

Industrial manufacturing also depends heavily on sensor fusion. A robotic arm assembling electronic devices may use cameras to identify component locations, force sensors to monitor gripping pressure, motion sensors to control precise movement, and laser measurement systems to verify accurate positioning. Artificial intelligence continuously compares information from all of these sensors to ensure each component is installed correctly. If one sensor reports unexpected information, AI can immediately slow production, inspect the problem, or alert human operators before defective products reach customers. This combination of sensors improves product quality while reducing waste and manufacturing costs.

Agriculture has become increasingly dependent on sensor fusion as farms adopt precision farming technologies. Satellites monitor crop growth across entire regions. Drones collect high-resolution images of individual fields. Soil moisture sensors measure water availability below the surface. Weather stations monitor rainfall, temperature, humidity, and wind conditions. GPS guides tractors with remarkable precision, while AI analyzes all of these data sources together. Instead of applying water or fertilizer evenly across an entire field, farmers can treat only the areas that need attention. This approach increases crop production while conserving water, reducing chemical use, and protecting the environment.

Sensor fusion is equally important in robotics. Imagine a humanoid robot assisting nurses inside a hospital. Cameras identify patients and recognize facial expressions. Microphones understand spoken requests. Touch sensors help the robot safely hand objects to patients. Motion sensors maintain balance while walking. GPS or indoor positioning systems help the robot navigate large buildings. Artificial intelligence combines all of this information continuously, allowing the robot to respond naturally and safely. If any single sensor temporarily fails, the robot can continue functioning because other sensors continue providing information.

One of the greatest strengths of sensor fusion is its ability to improve safety. Every sensor has limitations. Cameras struggle in darkness. Radar may not identify fine visual details. GPS signals may weaken inside tunnels or large buildings. Thermal cameras detect heat but not color. Microphones may be affected by loud background noise. Artificial intelligence recognizes these limitations and compensates by comparing information collected from multiple sources. Instead of trusting one sensor completely, AI evaluates all available evidence before making important decisions. This process significantly reduces the likelihood of errors while increasing confidence in the system's conclusions.

As artificial intelligence continues advancing, sensor fusion will become even more important. Future intelligent systems may combine hundreds or even thousands of different sensors operating simultaneously. Smart cities will integrate transportation, environmental monitoring, public safety, healthcare, energy systems, and communication networks into connected ecosystems. Space exploration missions will combine satellite observations, robotic sensors, scientific instruments, and autonomous navigation systems. Medical technologies will integrate wearable devices, genetic information, imaging systems, and continuous health monitoring. Artificial intelligence will organize these enormous streams of information into meaningful knowledge that helps people solve increasingly complex challenges.

Throughout this book, you have explored many individual sensing technologies. You have learned how AI sees, hears, touches, moves, navigates, observes invisible forms of energy, monitors Earth from space, and connects billions of devices through the Internet of Things. Sensor fusion represents the moment when all of these technologies come together. Intelligence is not created by one extraordinary sensor. It emerges when many different sensors work together, sharing information to create a richer, more complete understanding of the world. This ability to combine knowledge from many sources is one of the defining characteristics of modern artificial intelligence and one of the reasons AI continues transforming nearly every field of human activity.

Learn AI. Understand AI. Shape the Future.

— Susie Hala
IntelliGloss Press

Chapter 11 Summary

Chapter 11 introduced the concept of **sensor fusion**, one of the most important technologies in modern artificial intelligence. Students learned that AI becomes more intelligent not because of a single sensor, but because it combines information from many different sensors to develop a more complete understanding of its environment.

The chapter explained that every sensor has strengths and limitations. Cameras provide detailed visual information but may struggle in darkness or bad weather. Radar accurately measures speed and distance but cannot identify colors or facial expressions. GPS provides location but cannot detect nearby obstacles. Thermal cameras detect heat but cannot produce detailed color images. Rather than relying on one sensor, AI compares information collected from multiple sources to make safer and more accurate decisions.

Students explored several real-world examples of sensor fusion. Self-driving vehicles combine cameras, lidar, radar, GPS, and motion sensors to safely navigate roads. Hospitals use multiple medical devices to monitor patients and help physicians diagnose illnesses. Manufacturing robots combine cameras, pressure sensors, and motion sensors to assemble products with precision. Farmers use satellite imagery, drones, weather stations, and soil sensors to improve crop production while conserving resources.

The chapter also explained that sensor fusion improves safety by allowing AI to verify information before making decisions. If one sensor becomes blocked, damaged, or temporarily inaccurate, other sensors continue providing useful information. This redundancy helps intelligent systems operate more reliably in changing environments.

Finally, students learned that sensor fusion is becoming increasingly important as AI expands into transportation, healthcare, robotics, agriculture, smart cities, and space exploration. By combining information from many different sensors, AI develops a richer understanding of the world and becomes more capable of solving complex real-world problems.

Reflection

Every day, your brain performs sensor fusion without you realizing it. Your eyes, ears, skin, muscles, and balance system continuously collect information that your brain combines into one complete understanding of the world. Artificial intelligence follows a similar approach by combining information from cameras, microphones, GPS, lidar, radar, motion sensors, and many other technologies.

Learning about sensor fusion reminds us that intelligence is built from collaboration rather than isolation. No single sensor can understand everything. By combining multiple sources of information, AI becomes more accurate, reliable, and capable of making better decisions.

As intelligent systems continue expanding into homes, hospitals, schools, transportation, and industry, engineers must continue designing AI systems that use sensor fusion responsibly while protecting safety, privacy, and public trust.

Student Worksheet

Name: ______________________________________

Part A – Vocabulary

Define each term using your own words.

1. Sensor Fusion

____

____

2. Redundancy

____

____

3. Autonomous Vehicle

____

____

4. Artificial Intelligence

____

____

5. Decision-Making

Part B – Short Answer

1. What is sensor fusion?

2. Why is sensor fusion more reliable than using only one sensor?

3. Explain how self-driving vehicles use sensor fusion.

4. Give four industries that benefit from sensor fusion.

5. Why does sensor fusion improve safety?

Part C – Critical Thinking

Imagine you are designing an AI-powered robot to assist firefighters during emergency situations.

Write one paragraph explaining:

- Which sensors the robot should use.
- How sensor fusion would improve the robot's decision-making.
- Why combining multiple sensors would make the robot safer and more effective.

____
____
____
____
____
____
____

Chapter 11 Quiz

Multiple Choice

1. What is sensor fusion?

A. Using only one sensor to collect information

B. Combining information from multiple sensors to improve understanding

C. Connecting computers to the internet

D. Building larger robots

2. Why does AI use multiple sensors?

A. To make machines heavier

B. To improve accuracy and reliability

C. To increase electricity use

D. To reduce computer memory

3. Which group of sensors might be found in a self-driving vehicle?

A. Camera, lidar, radar, GPS, and motion sensors

B. Pencil, paper, and ruler

C. Flashlight and calculator

D. Television and radio

4. Which industry commonly uses sensor fusion to monitor patients?

A. Healthcare

B. Publishing

C. Banking

D. Retail clothing

5. What happens if one sensor becomes temporarily unreliable?

A. AI immediately shuts down.

B. Other sensors continue providing information to support decision-making.

C. AI ignores all information.

D. The computer permanently stops working.

True or False

6. _____ Every sensor has strengths and limitations.

7. _____ Sensor fusion helps AI make more accurate decisions.

8. _____ Self-driving vehicles rely on only one camera.

9. _____ Sensor fusion is used in agriculture, healthcare, manufacturing, and robotics.

10. _____ Combining multiple sensors improves reliability and safety.

Answer Key

Multiple Choice

1. **B** — Combining information from multiple sensors to improve understanding
2. **B** — To improve accuracy and reliability
3. **A** — Camera, lidar, radar, GPS, and motion sensors
4. **A** — Healthcare
5. **B** — Other sensors continue providing information to support decision-making.

True or False

6. **True**
7. **True**
8. **False**
9. **True**
10. **True**

Bonus Question

Imagine an autonomous delivery robot operating in a busy city.

Explain why it should combine information from cameras, lidar, radar, GPS, microphones, and motion sensors instead of relying on only one type of sensor.

Sample Answer:

Each sensor provides different information. Cameras identify objects and traffic signs, lidar creates three-dimensional maps, radar measures speed and distance, GPS determines location, microphones detect warning sounds such as emergency sirens, and motion sensors monitor balance and movement. By combining all of these data sources through sensor fusion, the robot can make safer, more accurate decisions while continuing to operate even if one sensor becomes temporarily less effective.

Classroom Discussion

1. Why is sensor fusion considered one of the most important technologies in artificial intelligence?
2. How does sensor fusion make self-driving vehicles safer?

3. Why do hospitals use multiple monitoring devices instead of relying on a single measurement?
4. How does sensor fusion improve robotics, agriculture, manufacturing, and environmental monitoring?
5. As AI systems become increasingly dependent on sensor fusion, what ethical responsibilities should engineers consider when designing systems that people trust with their safety and well-being?

Key Takeaways

After completing this chapter, you should be able to:

- Explain what sensor fusion is and why it is essential to artificial intelligence.
- Describe how AI combines information from multiple sensors to improve decision-making.
- Identify the strengths and limitations of individual sensors.
- Understand why redundancy increases the reliability and safety of intelligent systems.
- Recognize real-world applications of sensor fusion in transportation, healthcare, manufacturing, agriculture, robotics, and smart cities.
- Explain why combining multiple data sources allows AI to better understand complex environments.
- Appreciate that modern artificial intelligence achieves its greatest capabilities when many sensors work together to create a complete picture of the world.

Learn AI. Understand AI. Shape the Future.

— Susie Hala
IntelliGloss Press

Chapter 12

From Data to Decisions: How Artificial Intelligence Understands Information and Chooses Actions

Every second of every day, the world is filled with information. Cars move through busy intersections, students raise their hands in classrooms, doctors examine patients, airplanes fly across the sky, weather systems change, and millions of people communicate through phones and computers. Cameras capture images, microphones detect sounds, satellites observe the Earth, and sensors measure temperature, movement, pressure, and countless other conditions. Together, these technologies generate an enormous amount of data. However, collecting data alone does not create intelligence. A computer can store billions of numbers, photographs, and recordings without understanding what any of them mean. True intelligence begins only when information is organized, interpreted, and transformed into decisions. This is one of the most important responsibilities of artificial intelligence.

Throughout this book, you have learned how AI gathers information using many different types of sensors. Cameras allow AI to observe its surroundings. Microphones collect sound. Touch sensors measure physical contact. Motion sensors detect movement and balance. GPS provides location. Lidar, radar, infrared cameras, and satellites expand AI's ability to observe the world. Sensor fusion combines these different sources of information into a more complete picture of the environment. Yet one important question remains: **How does AI decide what to do next?** Understanding this process helps us see why artificial intelligence is much more than a collection of sensors. It is a decision-making system designed to analyze information and choose appropriate actions.

To understand AI decision-making, imagine a firefighter responding to an emergency. As the firefighter approaches a burning building, they immediately begin collecting information. They observe smoke rising from the roof, listen for people calling for help, feel the heat coming from nearby windows, notice the direction of the wind, and communicate with other emergency responders. None of these observations alone tells the entire story. The firefighter combines all of this information, compares it with previous experience and training, evaluates possible risks, and then decides how to respond. Artificial intelligence follows a similar process. It receives information from many different sensors, compares that information with patterns learned during training, evaluates possible actions, and selects the response that appears most appropriate for the situation.

One of the first steps in AI decision-making is **data processing**. Raw sensor data often contains far more information than AI actually needs. A digital camera may capture millions of pixels in a single image. A microphone records thousands of sound waves every second. GPS continuously updates location information, while motion sensors measure acceleration many times each second. Artificial intelligence begins by organizing this raw information into a form that computers can analyze more efficiently. This may include removing unnecessary data, correcting errors, improving image quality, reducing background noise, or combining measurements from multiple sensors. Processing prepares information for the next stage of intelligent analysis.

Once information has been organized, AI begins looking for **patterns**. Pattern recognition is one of the defining characteristics of artificial intelligence. Instead of examining every piece of information individually, AI searches for relationships that have been learned during training. For example, an AI system analyzing traffic may recognize that slowing vehicles, illuminated brake lights, and changing traffic signals often occur together before an intersection becomes congested. A medical AI may identify a combination of symptoms, laboratory results, and imaging findings that resemble previously diagnosed illnesses. A manufacturing robot may recognize vibration patterns that often appear before machinery begins to fail. These patterns help AI understand what is happening rather than simply recording isolated observations.

Artificial intelligence also depends heavily on **probability**. Humans often expect computers to produce perfect answers, but many AI systems operate by estimating the most likely outcome based on available information. Imagine looking outside and seeing dark clouds, strong winds, and falling temperatures. You might predict that rain is likely even before the first raindrop falls. You cannot know with complete certainty, but you can make a reasonable prediction based on the evidence. AI performs similar calculations by assigning probabilities to different possibilities. A medical system might estimate that a patient has a high probability of a particular illness. A self-driving vehicle may determine there is a very high probability that a pedestrian intends to cross the street. By calculating probabilities, AI can make informed decisions even when information is incomplete or uncertain.

After recognizing patterns and estimating probabilities, AI evaluates possible actions. This stage is often called **decision-making** because the system must choose among several alternatives. Consider a delivery robot traveling down a sidewalk. Suddenly, a group of children begins playing directly in its path. The robot could stop, slow down, turn slightly to avoid the group, or select an entirely different route. Artificial intelligence evaluates each option by considering safety, efficiency, and the likelihood of success. It then chooses the action that best satisfies its objectives. This process often occurs within fractions of a second, allowing intelligent systems to respond quickly to changing conditions.

Feedback plays an equally important role in AI decision-making. Humans constantly learn from experience. If a particular solution works well, we are more likely to use it again in the future. If it fails, we adjust our approach. Many AI systems improve in similar ways by comparing the results of their decisions with the outcomes that actually occur. If a recommendation successfully solves a problem, the system strengthens its confidence in similar decisions. If the outcome is poor, the AI adjusts its internal models to improve future performance. This ability to learn from feedback allows intelligent systems to become more accurate over time.

Decision-making also requires priorities. In many situations, AI must balance competing goals rather than pursuing only one objective. An autonomous vehicle should reach its destination efficiently, but safety must always remain the highest priority. A hospital scheduling system should reduce patient waiting times while ensuring that emergency cases receive immediate attention. An energy management system should reduce electricity costs without compromising the comfort or safety of building occupants. Artificial intelligence must evaluate these competing priorities before selecting the most appropriate course of action.

As AI becomes increasingly capable, responsible decision-making becomes even more important. Engineers must carefully design intelligent systems so that they operate fairly, transparently, and safely. AI decisions can affect transportation, healthcare, education, finance, manufacturing, agriculture, and many other areas of daily life. Because these decisions influence real people, developers must continually test AI systems, identify possible errors, reduce bias, and ensure that humans remain responsible for overseeing important decisions. Intelligence alone is not enough. Wisdom, accountability, and ethical responsibility are equally important when designing systems that people trust.

Throughout this book, you have seen how artificial intelligence observes the world through an extraordinary collection of sensors. In this chapter, you discovered that observation is only the beginning. True intelligence emerges when AI transforms information into understanding and understanding into action. Every recommendation made by a virtual assistant, every route selected by a navigation system, every medical alert generated by a hospital monitoring system, and every movement performed by a robot begins with the same process: collecting information, recognizing patterns, evaluating possibilities, and choosing the best available action. This ability to transform data into intelligent decisions lies at the very heart of artificial intelligence and will continue shaping the technologies that define the future.

Learn AI. Understand AI. Shape the Future.

— Susie Hala
IntelliGloss Press

Chapter 12 Summary

Chapter 12 explored one of the most important concepts in artificial intelligence: **how AI transforms data into intelligent decisions**. Students learned that collecting information is only the first step. Artificial intelligence becomes useful when it organizes data, recognizes patterns, evaluates possible solutions, and selects the best course of action.

The chapter explained that AI receives enormous amounts of information from cameras, microphones, GPS, motion sensors, touch sensors, satellites, and many other devices. Before making decisions, AI processes this raw information by removing unnecessary data, correcting errors, and organizing it into a form that computers can analyze efficiently.

Students learned that **pattern recognition** is one of AI's most powerful abilities. By studying millions of examples during training, AI learns to recognize relationships between different pieces of information. These patterns help AI identify objects, predict outcomes, recognize diseases, improve transportation, detect equipment failures, and solve many other real-world problems.

The chapter also introduced the concept of **probability**, explaining that AI often estimates the most likely outcome rather than providing absolute certainty. Just as people make decisions based on available evidence, AI evaluates probabilities before selecting the most appropriate action.

Students discovered that AI decision-making involves comparing multiple possible solutions while considering important priorities such as safety, efficiency, accuracy, and reliability. They also learned that AI improves over time by learning from feedback and adjusting its future decisions based on previous results.

Finally, the chapter emphasized that responsible AI requires human oversight. Engineers must design intelligent systems that are fair, transparent, safe, and ethical because AI decisions increasingly affect healthcare, education, transportation, business, agriculture, and many other aspects of society.

Reflection

Every decision we make begins with information. Humans constantly observe the world, recognize patterns, remember past experiences, and evaluate possible choices before taking action. Artificial intelligence follows a similar process by collecting data, organizing information, identifying patterns, calculating probabilities, and selecting actions based on what it has learned.

Learning about AI decision-making reminds us that intelligence is much more than collecting information. The true value of AI lies in its ability to transform information into knowledge that helps people solve problems more effectively. However, intelligent decisions also require responsibility. As AI becomes more involved in our daily lives, humans must continue guiding its development with fairness, transparency, accountability, and ethical principles.

Understanding how AI makes decisions prepares students to become informed users, responsible citizens, and future innovators who recognize both the incredible opportunities and the important responsibilities that come with artificial intelligence.

Student Worksheet

Name: ____

Part A – Vocabulary

Define each term using your own words.

1. Data Processing

____

____

2. Pattern Recognition

____

____

3. Probability

4. Decision-Making

5. Feedback

Part B – Short Answer

1. Why is collecting data only the first step in artificial intelligence?

2. Explain how AI uses pattern recognition to solve problems.

3. Why does AI use probability when making decisions?

4. How does feedback help AI improve over time?

5. Why is human oversight important when AI makes decisions?

Part C – Critical Thinking

Imagine you are helping design an AI system for a hospital emergency room.

Write one paragraph explaining:

- What information the AI should collect.
- How it would process that information.
- How it would help doctors make better decisions.
- Why humans should still make the final medical decisions.

Chapter 12 Quiz

Multiple Choice

1. What happens after AI collects information from sensors?

A. It immediately shuts down.

B. It processes and organizes the information.

C. It deletes the information.

D. It prints the information.

2. What is pattern recognition?

A. Decorating objects with designs.

B. Identifying relationships and similarities within data.

C. Building computer hardware.

D. Connecting to the internet.

3. Why does AI use probability?

A. To guess randomly.

B. To estimate the most likely outcome based on available information.

C. To increase computer speed.

D. To store larger files.

4. Which process helps AI improve its future decisions?

A. Ignoring mistakes.

B. Feedback and learning from previous outcomes.

C. Deleting all previous information.

D. Turning off the sensors.

5. Why should humans continue overseeing important AI decisions?

A. AI should never be monitored.

B. Important decisions require accountability, ethics, and human judgment.

C. AI cannot process information.

D. Computers cannot store data.

True or False

6. _____ Artificial intelligence first processes data before making decisions.

7. _____ Pattern recognition helps AI identify meaningful relationships in data.

8. _____ AI always provides perfect answers with complete certainty.

9. _____ Feedback allows AI systems to improve over time.

10. _____ Responsible AI development includes fairness, transparency, and human oversight.

Answer Key

Multiple Choice

1. **B** — It processes and organizes the information.
2. **B** — Identifying relationships and similarities within data.
3. **B** — To estimate the most likely outcome based on available information.
4. **B** — Feedback and learning from previous outcomes.
5. **B** — Important decisions require accountability, ethics, and human judgment.

True or False

6. **True**
7. **True**
8. **False**
9. **True**
10. **True**

Bonus Question

Imagine an autonomous vehicle approaches a busy intersection while it is raining heavily. The cameras have limited visibility, but the radar, lidar, GPS, and motion sensors continue providing information.

Explain how AI would use this information to make a safe driving decision.

Sample Answer:

The AI would combine information from all available sensors through sensor fusion. Radar would measure the speed and distance of nearby vehicles, lidar would create a three-dimensional map of the surroundings, GPS would identify the vehicle's location, and motion sensors would monitor acceleration and steering. By analyzing all of these data sources together, the AI could make a safer and more accurate decision than if it relied on the camera alone.

Classroom Discussion

1. Why is collecting data only the beginning of artificial intelligence?
2. How does pattern recognition help AI solve real-world problems?
3. Why do AI systems often calculate probabilities instead of giving absolute answers?
4. Why should humans continue supervising important AI decisions in healthcare, transportation, education, and finance?
5. As AI becomes more capable of making decisions, how can society ensure these systems remain fair, transparent, ethical, and trustworthy?

Key Takeaways

After completing this chapter, you should be able to:

- Explain how AI transforms raw data into intelligent decisions.
- Describe the roles of data processing, pattern recognition, probability, and feedback in AI.
- Understand why AI evaluates multiple possible actions before selecting the best response.
- Recognize how AI supports decision-making in healthcare, transportation, manufacturing, agriculture, and many other industries.
- Explain why feedback allows AI systems to continuously improve.
- Understand the importance of human oversight, ethics, and accountability in AI decision-making.
- Appreciate that artificial intelligence becomes truly valuable when it transforms information into knowledge that helps people solve real-world challenges responsibly.

Learn AI. Understand AI. Shape the Future.

— Susie Hala
IntelliGloss Press

Chapter 13

From Decisions to Action: How Artificial Intelligence Uses Actuators to Change the Physical World

Imagine standing in front of a light switch. Your eyes recognize the switch on the wall. Your brain decides that the room is too dark and needs more light. You reach out your hand, press the switch, and the lights turn on. Although this seems like a very simple activity, it actually involves several important steps working together. First, your senses collect information. Next, your brain processes that information and makes a decision. Finally, your muscles perform a physical action. Without that final step, nothing would happen. Knowing what to do is important, but taking action is what changes the world.

Artificial intelligence works in much the same way. Throughout this book, you have learned how AI collects information through cameras, microphones, touch sensors, motion sensors, GPS, satellites, and many other technologies. You have also discovered how AI processes information, recognizes patterns, combines data through sensor fusion, and makes intelligent decisions. However, one important question remains: **How does AI carry out those decisions?** The answer lies in a group of devices known as **actuators**. If sensors serve as the senses of artificial intelligence, actuators serve as its muscles. They transform digital decisions into physical actions that interact with the real world.

An **actuator** is a device that converts electrical signals into mechanical movement or physical action. Artificial intelligence itself cannot move objects directly because software exists only inside computers. Instead, AI sends commands to actuators, which perform the requested movement. Electric motors, hydraulic cylinders, pneumatic systems, robotic joints, valves, and many other mechanical devices act as actuators. Whenever a robot moves its arm, a drone changes direction, an automatic door opens, or a smart thermostat adjusts the temperature, actuators are performing the physical work while AI provides the instructions.

To better understand actuators, imagine a pianist performing a beautiful piece of music. The musician reads the notes, interprets the music, and decides which keys to press. However, the piano produces sound only because the musician's fingers physically move across the keyboard. Artificial intelligence functions similarly. The computer analyzes information and decides what should happen, but actuators perform the actual movement. Intelligence without action would remain only an idea inside a computer.

One of the most common actuators found in AI systems is the **electric motor**. Electric motors convert electrical energy into rotational movement. They power robotic arms in factories, drive the wheels of autonomous delivery robots, adjust mirrors in modern vehicles, control conveyor belts in warehouses, and move countless other mechanical systems. Artificial intelligence determines how fast the motor should turn, how far it should move, and when it should stop. Sensors continuously monitor the movement while AI makes tiny adjustments to ensure accuracy. This constant communication between sensors, AI, and actuators creates smooth and reliable operation.

Robotic arms provide an excellent example of how actuators work together. Imagine a manufacturing robot assembling smartphones. Cameras identify the location of each electronic component. Pressure sensors measure grip strength. Motion sensors monitor joint movement. Artificial intelligence determines the correct sequence of assembly. Finally, dozens of electric motors inside the robotic arm move each joint with incredible precision. The robot gently picks up a tiny electronic chip, rotates it into the correct position, and places it onto a circuit board with an accuracy measured in fractions of a millimeter. Every movement results from AI sending instructions to actuators that perform the physical work.

Actuators are equally important in healthcare. Modern surgical robots allow physicians to perform delicate procedures through very small incisions. Surgeons remain fully responsible for every decision, but robotic systems provide extraordinary precision by using actuators capable of movements much smaller than the human hand can easily perform. In rehabilitation medicine, powered prosthetic limbs use actuators to move artificial arms and legs according to the user's intentions. Hospital beds automatically adjust their position using electric actuators to improve patient comfort and safety. These examples demonstrate how AI and mechanical systems work together to improve healthcare without replacing the expertise of medical professionals.

Transportation provides another powerful example of AI action. Consider an autonomous vehicle approaching a red traffic light. Cameras recognize the traffic signal. GPS confirms the vehicle's location. Radar measures the distance to nearby vehicles. Artificial intelligence processes all of this information and decides that the vehicle must stop. The decision alone does not slow the car. Instead, AI sends commands to actuators controlling the braking system, steering, and electric motors. Within moments, the vehicle safely reduces speed and comes to a complete stop. This entire process—from sensing to decision-making to physical action—may occur in only a few seconds.

Smart homes also depend on actuators. When a smart thermostat determines that a room has become too warm, it sends commands to the heating and cooling system. Motorized window blinds automatically open or close throughout the day. Smart door locks secure entrances without human intervention. Irrigation systems water gardens according to weather conditions measured by environmental sensors. AI decides what should happen, while actuators carry out those decisions by controlling mechanical devices throughout the home.

Factories around the world increasingly rely on AI-powered automation. Conveyor belts move products between workstations using electric motors. Robotic arms assemble automobiles, package food, sort recyclable materials, and inspect manufactured goods. Automated warehouse systems retrieve products from storage shelves and deliver them to shipping stations. Artificial intelligence coordinates thousands of actuators working together to improve speed, accuracy, and efficiency while allowing human workers to focus on supervision, creativity, maintenance, and complex problem-solving.

One important feature of intelligent actuators is **feedback control**. Imagine throwing a basketball toward a hoop. As the ball travels through the air, your eyes observe its movement. If you miss the basket, your brain adjusts the next throw based on what you learned. Robots perform similar corrections using feedback systems. Sensors continuously monitor actuator movements while AI compares the actual movement with the desired movement. If the robotic arm moves too far or not far enough, AI immediately sends new instructions that correct the error. This continuous cycle of sensing, deciding, acting, and correcting allows intelligent machines to achieve remarkable precision.

Although actuators make AI capable of changing the physical world, they must always operate safely. Engineers carefully design emergency stop systems, protective barriers, collision detection sensors, and software safeguards that prevent dangerous movements. Collaborative robots, often called **cobots**, are specifically designed to work safely alongside human employees by continuously monitoring physical contact and immediately stopping if unexpected resistance is detected. These safety systems demonstrate that responsible engineering is just as important as technological innovation.

By now, you have explored nearly every stage of how intelligent systems operate. Sensors collect information. Artificial intelligence processes data, recognizes patterns, and makes decisions. Actuators transform those decisions into real-world actions. Together, these technologies form the complete cycle that allows AI to interact with people, machines, and the environment. Understanding actuators completes one of the most important lessons in artificial intelligence: intelligence is not measured only by the ability to think. True intelligence also includes the ability to act responsibly, accurately, and safely in the physical world.

Learn AI. Understand AI. Shape the Future.

— Susie Hala
IntelliGloss Press

Chapter 13 Summary

Chapter 13 introduced **actuators**, the devices that allow artificial intelligence to transform decisions into physical actions. Throughout the book, students have learned how AI collects information through sensors, processes data, recognizes patterns, and makes decisions. This chapter completed the AI decision cycle by explaining how AI carries out those decisions in the real world.

Students learned that **actuators** are mechanical or electronic devices that convert electrical signals into movement. If sensors serve as the eyes, ears, and other senses of AI, actuators serve as its muscles. They allow robots, autonomous vehicles, smart homes, factory machines, and many other intelligent systems to move, lift, rotate, open, close, grip, steer, and perform physical tasks.

The chapter explained how electric motors, hydraulic systems, pneumatic systems, robotic joints, and valves function as actuators in different industries. Students discovered how robotic arms assemble electronics with incredible precision, how surgical robots assist physicians during delicate procedures, and how autonomous vehicles use actuators to control steering, braking, and acceleration safely.

Students also explored the importance of **feedback control**, where sensors continuously monitor actuator movements while AI makes tiny adjustments to improve accuracy. This feedback loop allows intelligent machines to correct errors, maintain precision, and respond to changing environments in real time.

Finally, the chapter emphasized that intelligent action must always be accompanied by safety. Engineers design emergency stop systems, collision detection technologies, and collaborative robots that work safely alongside humans. Artificial intelligence becomes truly valuable when it not only makes intelligent decisions but also performs actions responsibly, accurately, and safely.

Reflection

Making good decisions is only part of intelligence. Acting on those decisions safely and responsibly is equally important. Humans constantly transform thoughts into actions by using muscles that respond to instructions from the brain. Artificial intelligence follows a similar process by using actuators that carry out instructions generated by AI systems.

Learning about actuators reminds us that intelligent machines are not simply computers that process information. They are complete systems capable of interacting with the physical world. Every robotic arm, autonomous vehicle, smart appliance, and medical robot depends on actuators working together with sensors and artificial intelligence.

As AI-powered machines become more common in homes, hospitals, factories, schools, and transportation systems, engineers must continue designing systems that place human safety, reliability, and ethical responsibility above speed or efficiency. Intelligence should always be used to improve people's lives while protecting those who depend on these technologies.

Student Worksheet

Name: ____

Part A – Vocabulary

Define each vocabulary word using your own words.

1. Actuator

---

2. Electric Motor

3. Feedback Control

4. Collaborative Robot (Cobot)

5. Automation

Part B – Short Answer

1. What is an actuator, and why is it important in artificial intelligence?

2. Explain how actuators are similar to human muscles.

3. Describe how sensors and actuators work together.

4. Give four examples of industries that use AI-powered actuators.

5. Why is feedback control important for intelligent machines?

Part C – Critical Thinking

Imagine you are designing an AI-powered robot to assist nurses in a hospital.

Write one paragraph explaining:

- What sensors the robot should use.
- What actuators it would need.
- How sensors, AI, and actuators would work together to safely assist patients.
- Why human supervision should remain important.

Chapter 13 Quiz

Multiple Choice

1. What is the primary purpose of an actuator?

A. To collect information

B. To convert AI decisions into physical actions

C. To store internet data

D. To measure temperature

2. If sensors are considered the "senses" of AI, actuators are often compared to what?

A. Eyes

B. Brain

C. Muscles

D. Ears

3. Which device commonly serves as an actuator in robotics?

A. Electric motor

B. GPS receiver

C. Camera

D. Microphone

4. What is feedback control?

A. Ignoring sensor information

B. Continuously monitoring movement and making corrections

C. Turning off the robot

D. Increasing internet speed

5. Why are collaborative robots (cobots) different from many traditional industrial robots?

A. They are designed to work safely alongside people.

B. They only operate underwater.

C. They cannot use sensors.

D. They do not require electricity.

True or False

6. _____ Actuators allow AI systems to physically interact with the environment.

7. _____ Sensors and actuators perform the same job.

8. _____ Feedback control helps improve movement accuracy.

9. _____ Autonomous vehicles use actuators for steering, braking, and acceleration.

10. _____ Safety systems are an important part of AI-powered machines.

Answer Key

Multiple Choice

1. **B** — To convert AI decisions into physical actions
2. **C** — Muscles
3. **A** — Electric motor
4. **B** — Continuously monitoring movement and making corrections
5. **A** — They are designed to work safely alongside people.

True or False

6. **True**
7. **False**
8. **True**
9. **True**
10. **True**

Bonus Question

Imagine an autonomous warehouse robot receives instructions to move a package from one location to another.

Explain how the complete AI cycle works from beginning to end.

Sample Answer:

The robot's cameras, GPS, motion sensors, and obstacle sensors collect information about its surroundings. Artificial intelligence processes the data, recognizes obstacles, identifies the package, and plans the safest route. The AI then sends commands to actuators, including electric motors and robotic arms, which move the robot, lift the package, and transport it to its destination. Throughout the process, sensors continuously provide feedback so AI can adjust movements and avoid collisions, completing the full cycle of **Sense → Process → Decide → Act**.

Classroom Discussion

1. Why are actuators considered the "muscles" of artificial intelligence?
2. How do sensors, AI, and actuators work together to complete intelligent tasks?
3. Why is feedback control essential for robots and autonomous vehicles?
4. How are actuators improving healthcare, manufacturing, transportation, and smart homes?
5. As AI-powered machines become more capable of acting independently, what responsibilities do engineers have to ensure these systems remain safe, reliable, and beneficial to society?

Key Takeaways

After completing this chapter, you should be able to:

- Explain what actuators are and why they are essential to artificial intelligence.
- Describe how actuators convert AI decisions into physical actions.
- Understand the relationship between sensors, artificial intelligence, and actuators.
- Identify common types of actuators, including electric motors, hydraulic systems, and pneumatic systems.
- Explain the purpose of feedback control in improving movement accuracy.
- Recognize real-world applications of actuators in robotics, healthcare, transportation, manufacturing, and smart homes.
- Appreciate that intelligent action requires not only advanced technology but also safety, responsibility, and ethical engineering.

Learn AI. Understand AI. Shape the Future.

— Susie Hala
IntelliGloss Press

Chapter 14

Learning from Experience: How Artificial Intelligence Improves Through Feedback and Adaptation

Think about the first time you learned to ride a bicycle. At first, everything felt unfamiliar. You struggled to keep your balance, your steering was uncertain, and you may have fallen several times before successfully riding on your own. Each mistake, however, taught you something valuable. You learned how much to turn the handlebars, when to apply the brakes, how to shift your body weight, and how to maintain balance while moving forward. Over time, what once seemed impossible became almost automatic. Today, many people can ride a bicycle without consciously thinking about every movement because their brains have learned through practice and experience.

Artificial intelligence improves in a similar way. Although computers do not experience the world as humans do, many AI systems become better over time by learning from information, evaluating results, and adjusting future decisions. Throughout this book, you have discovered how AI collects information through sensors, combines data using sensor fusion, makes decisions, and performs actions through actuators. However, intelligent systems do not simply repeat the same actions forever. Many modern AI systems continuously evaluate their performance and use feedback to improve accuracy, efficiency, and reliability. This ability to adapt is one of the defining characteristics that separates modern artificial intelligence from traditional computer programs.

Traditional software follows instructions exactly as programmers write them. If a calculator is programmed to add two numbers, it performs the same calculation every time without learning anything new. Artificial intelligence is different because many AI systems adjust their internal models after analyzing the results of previous decisions. Instead of remaining fixed, they gradually improve by identifying successful patterns while reducing errors. This process allows AI to perform many tasks with increasing accuracy as it gains additional experience.

One of the most important concepts in AI improvement is **feedback**. Feedback is information that tells a system how well it performed a particular task. Humans receive feedback constantly. A teacher returns a graded assignment with comments explaining strengths and areas for improvement. A basketball player watches whether the ball goes through the hoop. A musician listens carefully while practicing an instrument. Every piece of feedback helps people refine their skills. Artificial intelligence follows a similar process. After making a prediction or performing an action, AI compares the result with the desired outcome. If the result is accurate, the system strengthens the patterns that produced success. If the result contains errors, AI adjusts its internal calculations to improve future performance.

Imagine an AI system that helps doctors identify signs of pneumonia in chest X-rays. During training, the AI analyzes thousands of medical images that have already been carefully reviewed by experienced radiologists. At first, the AI may incorrectly classify some images. Each mistake provides valuable feedback. The system compares its prediction with the correct diagnosis and adjusts its mathematical model. After repeating this process many thousands of times, the AI becomes much more accurate because it has learned from previous errors. Although the system is not "thinking" like a physician, it is improving its ability to recognize important visual patterns.

Feedback also plays a critical role in robotics. Imagine a robotic arm assembling delicate electronic components inside a manufacturing plant. Sensors monitor the position of each part while pressure sensors measure grip strength. If the robot places a component slightly out of position, cameras immediately detect the error. Artificial intelligence analyzes the feedback, calculates the correction, and slightly adjusts future movements. These tiny improvements occur continuously, allowing the robot to become more precise over time while reducing manufacturing defects.

Autonomous vehicles provide another excellent example of learning through feedback. Every trip generates enormous amounts of information. Cameras observe road conditions, radar measures nearby vehicles, lidar creates three-dimensional maps, GPS records location, and motion sensors monitor acceleration and steering. AI analyzes this information to evaluate how well it handled lane changes, braking, obstacle avoidance, and navigation. Engineers use these observations to improve future software updates, allowing autonomous systems to become safer and more reliable as they encounter new driving situations.

Feedback is also essential in education. Many online learning platforms now use artificial intelligence to personalize instruction for individual students. As learners answer questions, complete assignments, or solve problems, AI evaluates their performance. If a student struggles with a particular concept, the system may provide additional examples, simpler explanations, or extra practice. If the student demonstrates mastery, AI introduces more advanced material. Rather than treating every learner exactly the same, intelligent educational systems adapt instruction to meet individual learning needs. This personalized approach helps students learn more efficiently while giving teachers additional tools to support classroom instruction.

Another important idea is **adaptation**. Adaptation means changing behavior in response to new information or changing conditions. Humans constantly adapt. We carry umbrellas when rain is forecast, wear warmer clothing during winter, and take different routes when roads become congested. Artificial intelligence also adapts by responding to changes in its environment. Smart thermostats learn household schedules and adjust temperatures automatically. Traffic management systems modify traffic signals based on congestion. Energy systems balance electricity production according to changing demand. These adaptive systems help improve efficiency while responding intelligently to changing circumstances.

Learning, however, does not happen automatically. Artificial intelligence depends on high-quality data, careful engineering, and responsible human oversight. If AI learns from incomplete, inaccurate, or biased information, it may develop incorrect patterns that produce poor decisions. For this reason, engineers carefully evaluate training data, monitor system performance, and regularly update AI models to maintain accuracy and fairness. Continuous improvement requires continuous responsibility.

As AI becomes increasingly capable, learning from experience will become even more important. Future robots may adapt to unfamiliar environments while exploring distant planets. Medical AI systems may identify new diseases by recognizing emerging patterns in patient data. Environmental monitoring systems may improve their ability to predict wildfires, floods, and severe storms. Educational AI may provide increasingly personalized learning experiences for students around the world. In every case, improvement depends on the same fundamental process: collecting information, receiving feedback, learning from experience, and adapting future behavior.

By now, you have explored nearly every major stage of how intelligent systems operate. Artificial intelligence observes the world through sensors, processes information, makes decisions, performs actions, and learns from the results. This continuous cycle of sensing, thinking, acting, and improving allows AI to become increasingly capable over time. Understanding this process helps us appreciate that intelligence is not a single event but an ongoing journey of learning and adaptation. Just as people continue learning throughout their lives, many AI systems also improve through experience, helping them better serve humanity while opening new possibilities for the future.

Learn AI. Understand AI. Shape the Future.

— Susie Hala
IntelliGloss Press

Chapter 14 Summary

Chapter 14 explored how **artificial intelligence learns from experience through feedback and adaptation**. Students learned that unlike traditional computer programs, many AI systems improve their performance over time by analyzing results, recognizing mistakes, and adjusting future decisions based on new information.

The chapter explained that AI learning begins after data has been collected, processed, and used to make a decision. By comparing the outcome of its decision with the desired result, AI receives **feedback** that helps determine whether its actions were successful or need improvement. This process allows AI systems to become more accurate and reliable as they gain additional experience.

Students learned that **feedback** is one of the most important parts of artificial intelligence. Just as people learn from teachers, coaches, parents, and personal experience, AI systems learn by evaluating the results of previous decisions. Medical AI improves by analyzing correctly diagnosed patient cases. Manufacturing robots become more precise by correcting small positioning errors. Autonomous vehicles improve through the analysis of driving data collected during real-world testing.

The chapter also introduced the concept of **adaptation**, which allows AI to respond to changing situations instead of always behaving the same way. Smart thermostats adjust temperatures based on family routines. Educational software personalizes lessons based on student performance. Traffic management systems adjust traffic signals as road conditions change throughout the day.

Finally, students learned that AI learning requires responsible human supervision. Engineers must provide accurate training data, carefully monitor AI performance, reduce bias, and ensure that intelligent systems remain fair, safe, transparent, and beneficial to society. Learning makes AI more capable, but responsible oversight ensures that these capabilities are used wisely.

Reflection

Learning is a lifelong process. Every experience teaches us something new, helping us improve our knowledge, skills, and decision-making. Artificial intelligence follows a similar principle by learning from feedback, recognizing patterns, and adapting to new information over time.

Understanding AI learning reminds us that intelligence is not simply about having information. True intelligence involves continuously improving through experience while remaining open to new knowledge and changing conditions.

As AI becomes increasingly involved in healthcare, education, transportation, business, and many other fields, society must ensure that intelligent systems continue learning in ways that are fair, ethical, transparent, and beneficial for everyone. Human guidance remains essential because technology should always serve humanity's best interests.

Student Worksheet

Name: ______________________________________

Part A – Vocabulary

Define each vocabulary word using your own words.

1. Feedback

____

____

2. Adaptation

____

3. Machine Learning

4. Training Data

5. Continuous Improvement

Part B – Short Answer

1. Why is feedback important in artificial intelligence?

2. How does AI improve after making mistakes?

3. Explain the difference between traditional computer programs and AI systems that learn.

4. Give four examples of AI systems that improve through feedback.

5. Why should humans continue supervising AI learning?

Part C – Critical Thinking

Imagine you are designing an AI tutoring system for middle school students.

Write one paragraph explaining:

- How the AI would collect feedback from students.
- How it would adapt future lessons.
- How teachers would continue supervising the learning process.
- Why personalized learning could improve education.

Chapter 14 Quiz

Multiple Choice

1. What helps artificial intelligence improve over time?

A. Feedback

B. Electricity

C. Paper

D. Paint

2. What does adaptation mean?

A. Never changing.

B. Changing behavior based on new information or changing conditions.

C. Turning off the computer.

D. Printing documents.

3. Which statement best describes traditional computer programs?

A. They automatically improve from experience.

B. They follow programmed instructions without learning on their own.

C. They build robots.

D. They replace teachers.

4. Which example demonstrates AI learning through feedback?

A. A medical AI improving after comparing its diagnosis with confirmed patient results.

B. A calculator adding numbers.

C. A flashlight turning on.

D. A printer making copies.

5. Why is high-quality training data important?

A. It helps AI learn accurate and reliable patterns.

B. It increases electricity use.

C. It makes computers heavier.

D. It removes sensors.

True or False

6. _____ AI can improve by learning from previous results.

7. _____ Feedback helps AI identify mistakes and improve future decisions.

8. _____ Traditional computer programs automatically learn from experience.

9. _____ Human supervision remains important for responsible AI development.

10. _____ Adaptation allows AI to respond to changing environments.

Answer Key

Multiple Choice

1. **A** — Feedback
2. **B** — Changing behavior based on new information or changing conditions
3. **B** — They follow programmed instructions without learning on their own.
4. **A** — A medical AI improving after comparing its diagnosis with confirmed patient results.
5. **A** — It helps AI learn accurate and reliable patterns.

True or False

6. **True**
7. **True**
8. **False**
9. **True**
10. **True**

Bonus Question

Imagine an AI system that helps farmers monitor crop health.

Explain how the complete learning cycle works from collecting information to improving future recommendations.

Sample Answer:

The AI collects information from satellites, drones, soil sensors, weather stations, and field equipment. It processes the data, identifies patterns that may indicate healthy or unhealthy crops, and recommends actions such as watering or applying fertilizer. Farmers then observe the results and provide feedback about whether the recommendations were successful. AI uses this feedback to improve its future predictions and recommendations, becoming more accurate over time while helping farmers increase crop production and conserve resources.

Classroom Discussion

1. Why is feedback one of the most important parts of artificial intelligence?
2. How is AI learning similar to the way humans learn new skills?
3. Why is adaptation important in rapidly changing environments?
4. How can AI improve education, healthcare, transportation, and agriculture by learning from experience?
5. As AI systems continue learning throughout their operation, what responsibilities do engineers, governments, educators, and businesses have to ensure these systems remain fair, safe, transparent, and accountable?

Key Takeaways

After completing this chapter, you should be able to:

- Explain how artificial intelligence improves through feedback and adaptation.
- Describe the role of feedback in helping AI recognize mistakes and improve future decisions.
- Understand the difference between traditional computer programs and AI systems that learn.
- Identify real-world applications of AI learning in healthcare, education, transportation, manufacturing, and agriculture.
- Explain why high-quality training data is essential for reliable AI performance.
- Recognize the importance of human oversight in monitoring AI learning and reducing bias.
- Appreciate that artificial intelligence is a continuously evolving technology that becomes more capable through experience while requiring responsible guidance from the people who design and use it.

Learn AI. Understand AI. Shape the Future.

— Susie Hala
IntelliGloss Press

Chapter 15

Artificial Intelligence and Human Intelligence: Comparing Artificial Senses with Human Perception

Throughout this book, you have explored the remarkable technologies that allow artificial intelligence to observe, understand, and interact with the world. You have learned how AI uses cameras to see, microphones to hear, tactile sensors to detect touch, motion sensors to measure movement, GPS to determine location, satellites to observe Earth, and advanced technologies such as lidar, radar, thermal imaging, and hyperspectral sensors to gather information beyond normal human vision. You have also discovered how artificial intelligence combines these different sources of information through sensor fusion, transforms data into decisions, carries out actions using actuators, and improves through feedback and learning. These capabilities demonstrate that AI has become an extraordinary technological achievement. Yet an important question remains: **Can artificial intelligence truly perceive the world the same way humans do?**

To answer this question, we must first understand what human perception really is. Human perception is much more than receiving information through the five traditional senses. Every second, your brain combines sight, hearing, touch, smell, taste, balance, body position, memory, emotions, language, previous experiences, and reasoning into one continuous understanding of the world. When you recognize a friend's face, you do more than identify physical features. You remember conversations, recognize their voice, recall shared experiences, understand emotions expressed through facial expressions, and often predict what they may say or do next. Human perception is deeply connected to memory, learning, relationships, emotions, and consciousness.

Artificial intelligence approaches perception differently. AI does not experience the world through feelings, memories, or personal awareness. Instead, it analyzes enormous amounts of data collected by sensors and searches for mathematical patterns. When a facial recognition system identifies a person, it compares measurable characteristics such as distances between the eyes, nose, mouth, and jawline with patterns stored in its training data. It does not recognize friendships, family relationships, or personal memories. AI recognizes patterns, while humans recognize meaning.

One of the greatest strengths of artificial intelligence is its ability to process enormous amounts of information with incredible speed. A human doctor may examine dozens of medical images during a busy workday, carefully studying each one before reaching a diagnosis. AI can analyze thousands of images within minutes while highlighting areas that deserve closer attention. Financial institutions use AI to examine millions of transactions every day for signs of fraud. Environmental scientists analyze decades of satellite imagery to monitor climate change. Astronomers use AI to study enormous amounts of telescope data while searching for distant galaxies and planets. In these situations, AI provides capabilities far beyond normal human speed and capacity.

However, speed does not always equal understanding. Imagine reading a novel about a young athlete overcoming tremendous obstacles to achieve success. As you read, you may feel excitement, disappointment, hope, sadness, and inspiration. You understand the motivations of the characters and recognize lessons that apply to your own life. Artificial intelligence can summarize the story, identify major themes, and answer questions about the plot, but it does not personally experience emotions or understand the story in the same deeply personal way that a human reader does. Human understanding includes emotional awareness, empathy, creativity, and lived experience—qualities that remain difficult to reproduce with today's AI systems.

Creativity provides another interesting comparison between humans and artificial intelligence. AI can generate artwork, compose music, write stories, create computer code, and design new products by learning patterns from enormous collections of existing examples. These abilities have transformed many industries by helping people work more efficiently and explore new ideas. Yet human creativity often begins with personal experiences, imagination, curiosity, cultural traditions, and emotional expression. A composer may write music inspired by family memories. An artist may create a painting that reflects joy, grief, or hope. A scientist may pursue a discovery because of curiosity about the natural world. AI can assist creative work, but human creativity often grows from experiences that extend beyond data alone.

Another important difference involves **common sense**. Humans naturally understand many everyday situations because we have spent our entire lives interacting with the physical world. For example, a child quickly learns that ice is slippery, fire is hot, and glass can break if dropped. We develop this knowledge through direct experience and observation. Artificial intelligence must often learn these relationships from carefully prepared data or repeated training. Although AI has become increasingly capable of reasoning about many situations, developing broad common-sense understanding across every aspect of daily life remains one of the greatest challenges in artificial intelligence research.

Ethics and values also highlight an important distinction between human and artificial intelligence. People constantly make decisions influenced by fairness, kindness, honesty, responsibility, compassion, and cultural values. These principles guide how we treat others and help us resolve difficult situations where there may not be one perfect answer. Artificial intelligence does not possess its own moral beliefs or personal values. Instead, it follows objectives, rules, and guidelines established by the people who design and deploy these systems. This is why human oversight remains essential whenever AI is used in areas such as healthcare, education, law, finance, public safety, and government. Technology can assist decision-making, but people remain responsible for ensuring those decisions are ethical and aligned with society's values.

The future will likely involve collaboration rather than competition between humans and artificial intelligence. Doctors may use AI to identify diseases more quickly while continuing to provide compassionate patient care. Teachers may use AI to personalize lessons while inspiring curiosity, confidence, and character development in their students. Engineers may use AI to design safer buildings and more efficient transportation systems while applying human judgment to solve complex problems. Scientists may rely on AI to analyze enormous amounts of research data while asking creative questions that lead to new discoveries. In each of these examples, AI serves as a powerful partner rather than a replacement for human intelligence.

Understanding both the strengths and limitations of artificial intelligence helps us become wiser users of technology. AI excels at processing enormous datasets, recognizing patterns, performing repetitive calculations, and supporting decision-making. Humans excel at empathy, creativity, ethical reasoning, imagination, leadership, and understanding the deeper meaning behind experiences. The greatest opportunities arise when these complementary strengths work together. By combining human wisdom with artificial intelligence, society can address challenges that neither humans nor machines could solve as effectively alone.

As you prepare to read the final chapter of this book, remember that artificial intelligence is not simply about building smarter machines. It is about helping people solve meaningful problems, improve lives, expand scientific knowledge, and create a better future. Understanding AI begins with understanding ourselves. The more we learn about how humans think, perceive, learn, and make decisions, the better prepared we will be to design intelligent technologies that reflect our highest values. The future of AI will not be shaped by technology alone—it will be shaped by the choices, creativity, and responsibility of the people who build and use it.

Learn AI. Understand AI. Shape the Future.

— Susie Hala
IntelliGloss Press

Chapter 15 Summary

Chapter 15 explored the similarities and differences between **artificial intelligence and human intelligence**. Students learned that although AI can process enormous amounts of information quickly and accurately, human intelligence includes qualities such as emotions, creativity, empathy, ethics, common sense, and personal experiences that today's AI does not possess.

The chapter explained that both humans and AI collect information from their environments, but they do so in different ways. Humans rely on their senses, memories, emotions, and life experiences to understand the world. Artificial intelligence depends on sensors, algorithms, training data, and mathematical models to recognize patterns and make predictions. While AI excels at processing large amounts of data, human intelligence provides deeper understanding, personal meaning, and moral judgment.

Students also learned that AI is extremely effective at identifying patterns, analyzing medical images, detecting fraud, interpreting satellite data, and supporting scientific research. However, AI does not experience emotions, build personal relationships, or understand the world through lived experiences. These human qualities continue to play an essential role in decision-making, creativity, leadership, and ethical reasoning.

The chapter emphasized that AI should not be viewed as a replacement for human intelligence but as a powerful tool that works alongside people. Doctors, teachers, scientists, engineers, business leaders, and many other professionals can use AI to improve productivity and solve complex problems while continuing to apply human judgment, compassion, and responsibility.

Finally, students learned that the future of artificial intelligence will depend on collaboration between humans and machines. By combining the strengths of AI with uniquely human qualities such as creativity, empathy, critical thinking, and ethical decision-making, society can develop technologies that improve lives while reflecting our shared values.

Reflection

Artificial intelligence has become one of the most powerful technologies ever created, but it is important to remember that intelligence is more than speed and computation. Human intelligence includes imagination, emotions, relationships, cultural understanding, and moral responsibility—qualities that shape how we solve problems and care for one another.

Learning about the differences between AI and human intelligence reminds us that technology should be designed to support people rather than replace them. AI can help analyze information, identify patterns, and improve efficiency, but humans remain responsible for making ethical decisions, showing compassion, and using wisdom when applying technology in everyday life.

The future will be strongest when humans and artificial intelligence work together, combining the speed of machines with the creativity, values, and judgment that make us uniquely human.

Student Worksheet

Name: ______________________________________

Part A – Vocabulary

Define each vocabulary word using your own words.

1. Human Intelligence

____

____

2. Artificial Intelligence

____

3. Empathy

4. Common Sense

5. Ethical Decision-Making

Part B – Short Answer

1. What is one major difference between artificial intelligence and human intelligence?

2. Why is human judgment still important when using AI?

3. List four tasks that AI performs exceptionally well.

4. Name four qualities that make human intelligence unique.

5. Why is collaboration between humans and AI important for the future?

____
____
____
____

Part C – Critical Thinking

Imagine you are part of a team developing AI for a children's hospital.

Write one paragraph explaining:

- How AI could help doctors and nurses.
- What decisions should always remain under human responsibility.
- Why empathy and compassion are important in healthcare.
- How humans and AI can work together to provide the best care for patients.

____
____
____
____
____
____
____

Chapter 15 Quiz

Multiple Choice

1. Which statement best describes artificial intelligence?

A. AI experiences emotions just like humans.

B. AI recognizes patterns and processes information using data and algorithms.

C. AI replaces all human thinking.

D. AI never makes mistakes.

2. Which quality is unique to human intelligence?

A. Processing billions of calculations every second

B. Empathy and emotional understanding

C. Reading digital data

D. Measuring temperature

3. What is one strength of artificial intelligence?

A. Feeling emotions

B. Analyzing large amounts of information quickly

C. Developing personal memories

D. Creating moral values

4. Why is human oversight important?

A. AI should never be monitored.

B. Humans provide ethical judgment, accountability, and responsibility.

C. AI cannot process information.

D. Computers cannot use sensors.

5. What is the best way to describe the future relationship between humans and AI?

A. AI will replace all people.

B. Humans and AI will work together by combining their strengths.

C. Humans will stop learning.

D. AI will eliminate creativity.

True or False

6. _____ Human intelligence includes emotions, empathy, and life experiences.

7. _____ AI recognizes mathematical patterns in data.

8. _____ AI understands personal memories exactly as humans do.

9. _____ Human creativity and ethical reasoning remain important in the age of AI.

10. _____ AI works best when it supports human decision-making instead of replacing it.

Answer Key

Multiple Choice

1. **B** — AI recognizes patterns and processes information using data and algorithms.
2. **B** — Empathy and emotional understanding
3. **B** — Analyzing large amounts of information quickly
4. **B** — Humans provide ethical judgment, accountability, and responsibility.
5. **B** — Humans and AI will work together by combining their strengths.

True or False

6. **True**
7. **True**
8. **False**
9. **True**
10. **True**

Bonus Question

Imagine a doctor is using an AI system to help diagnose a patient.

Explain how both the AI and the doctor contribute to providing the best possible care.

Sample Answer:

The AI quickly analyzes medical images, laboratory results, and patient data to identify patterns that may indicate a disease or medical condition. The doctor reviews the AI's findings, examines the patient, asks questions about symptoms and medical history, considers emotional and social factors, and makes the final treatment decision. By combining AI's speed and pattern recognition with the doctor's experience, empathy, and ethical judgment, patients receive more accurate and compassionate care.

Classroom Discussion

1. How do artificial intelligence and human intelligence work differently?
2. Why are empathy, creativity, and ethics difficult for AI to fully replicate?
3. In what ways can AI improve education, healthcare, transportation, and scientific research without replacing human expertise?
4. Why is it important for humans to remain responsible for decisions that affect people's lives?
5. As AI continues advancing, how can future generations ensure that technology reflects human values such as fairness, compassion, honesty, and responsibility?

Key Takeaways

After completing this chapter, you should be able to:

- Compare the strengths and limitations of artificial intelligence and human intelligence.
- Explain how humans and AI process information differently.
- Identify uniquely human qualities such as empathy, creativity, common sense, and ethical reasoning.
- Describe the strengths of AI in pattern recognition, data analysis, and problem-solving.
- Explain why human oversight remains essential in important decisions.
- Understand the importance of collaboration between humans and AI.
- Appreciate that the future of artificial intelligence depends not only on technological advancement but also on the wisdom, responsibility, and values of the people who design and use it.

Learn AI. Understand AI. Shape the Future.

— Susie Hala
IntelliGloss Press

Chapter 16

The Future of Artificial Intelligence: Building a Smarter World Together

When you first opened this book, you began an exciting journey into one of the most fascinating technologies ever created. At the beginning, you learned that artificial intelligence is much more than computers performing calculations. AI is a system that gathers information, understands its environment, makes decisions, takes action, and improves through experience. As you continued reading, you discovered that intelligent machines rely on many different sensors that function much like human senses. Cameras became AI's eyes, microphones became its ears, touch sensors allowed machines to feel pressure, motion sensors measured movement, GPS provided location, and advanced technologies such as lidar, radar, thermal imaging, satellites, and hyperspectral sensors expanded AI's ability to observe the world beyond normal human perception. Each chapter revealed another piece of a much larger picture, showing that intelligence is created when many technologies work together toward a common purpose.

One of the most important lessons from this book is that artificial intelligence does not begin with intelligence—it begins with **information**. Just as humans depend on their senses to understand the world, AI depends on sensors to collect data from its surroundings. Without information, intelligent systems cannot learn, recognize patterns, or make decisions. Every photograph captured by a camera, every sound detected by a microphone, every location measured by GPS, and every temperature recorded by a thermal sensor becomes part of the knowledge that AI uses to understand the environment. This simple idea forms the foundation of nearly every intelligent system operating today.

As you explored sensor fusion, smart cities, satellites, the Internet of Things, actuators, and adaptive learning, you discovered that artificial intelligence is not a single machine or computer program. It is an entire ecosystem of technologies working together. Thousands of sensors continuously collect information while communication networks connect billions of devices across the globe. Artificial intelligence analyzes enormous streams of data, identifies meaningful patterns, predicts future events, and supports decisions that affect healthcare, education, agriculture, transportation, manufacturing, scientific research, and environmental protection. Every new sensor added to this ecosystem expands AI's ability to observe and understand the world.

One of the most exciting discoveries in modern artificial intelligence is that machines are becoming increasingly capable of helping people solve problems that once seemed impossible. AI assists doctors in identifying diseases earlier than ever before. Scientists use AI to analyze enormous amounts of climate data while studying changes affecting our planet. Farmers produce more food while conserving water and fertilizer through precision agriculture. Engineers design safer vehicles and smarter transportation systems. Emergency responders receive valuable information during hurricanes, earthquakes, floods, and wildfires. Teachers use AI to personalize instruction while helping students learn at their own pace. These examples demonstrate that AI is already improving lives in ways that many people experience every day, often without realizing it.

However, technology alone cannot solve every problem. Throughout history, every important scientific discovery has brought both opportunities and responsibilities. Electricity transformed society but required safe electrical systems. Automobiles improved transportation but required traffic laws and driver's education. The internet connected billions of people but introduced new challenges involving privacy, cybersecurity, and misinformation. Artificial intelligence is no different. The same technologies that help doctors diagnose diseases can also raise questions about protecting patient privacy. AI systems that improve public safety must also respect individual rights and freedoms. Intelligent machines that automate routine tasks create opportunities for innovation while encouraging people to develop new skills for the future workforce. Every technological advancement requires thoughtful leadership and responsible decision-making.

This is why **ethics** plays such an important role in artificial intelligence. Ethical AI means designing intelligent systems that are fair, transparent, reliable, accountable, and beneficial to society. Engineers must carefully examine the data used to train AI systems to reduce bias and improve fairness. Governments establish laws and regulations that encourage innovation while protecting public safety. Businesses develop security measures that protect sensitive information from cyberattacks. Teachers help students learn how to use AI responsibly rather than depending on it for every answer. Families discuss how technology should be used wisely at home. Building trustworthy AI requires cooperation among scientists, engineers, educators, policymakers, businesses, and citizens working together toward shared goals.

As you think about your own future, remember that you are growing up during one of the most important technological transformations in human history. Previous generations witnessed the invention of electricity, airplanes, television, computers, and the internet. Your generation will help shape the future of artificial intelligence. Some of you may become engineers designing new AI systems. Others may become teachers using AI to improve education, doctors using AI to provide better healthcare, scientists exploring space with intelligent robots, artists creating new forms of digital creativity, entrepreneurs building innovative companies, or public leaders developing policies that guide responsible AI development. Even if you never write a single line of computer code, understanding how AI works will help you make informed decisions throughout your life.

One of the greatest opportunities of the future will be learning how humans and artificial intelligence can work together. Throughout this book, you discovered that AI has many remarkable strengths. It can analyze enormous amounts of information, recognize complex patterns, process data at incredible speed, and assist people in solving difficult problems. Humans contribute equally important strengths, including creativity, empathy, ethical reasoning, curiosity, leadership, imagination, communication, and the ability to understand the deeper meaning behind experiences. These strengths are not competitors—they are complementary. The future will belong to people who understand how to combine human intelligence with artificial intelligence to solve challenges that neither could solve as effectively alone.

Another lesson you should remember is that learning never ends. Artificial intelligence continues improving through feedback, adaptation, and new discoveries. People learn in much the same way. Every question you ask, every book you read, every experiment you perform, every mistake you correct, and every challenge you overcome adds to your knowledge and experience. Curiosity has always been one of humanity's greatest strengths. The desire to ask questions, seek understanding, and explore the unknown has driven every major scientific breakthrough throughout history. Artificial intelligence is simply the latest chapter in that ongoing story of discovery.

As AI continues evolving toward more advanced systems, the need for knowledgeable, thoughtful, and responsible leaders will continue growing. Understanding AI will become an essential skill for students entering nearly every profession. Whether you choose healthcare, engineering, education, law, agriculture, business, environmental science, public service, or another career, artificial intelligence will likely become one of the tools you use. The goal is not simply to know how AI works but to understand when to use it, how to evaluate its results, and how to ensure it serves people fairly and responsibly.

As you close this book, remember that artificial intelligence is ultimately a human achievement. Behind every intelligent system are people asking questions, solving problems, testing ideas, improving designs, and working together to create technologies that benefit society. The future of AI will not be determined only by faster computers or more advanced algorithms. It will be shaped by the character, wisdom, creativity, integrity, and compassion of the people who build and use these technologies.

Perhaps the most important lesson of all is this: **Artificial intelligence does not define the future—you do.** AI is a powerful tool, but tools are guided by the people who use them. The future belongs to curious learners who continue asking questions, exploring new ideas, thinking critically, solving problems responsibly, and working together to improve the world. Whether you become an inventor, teacher, engineer, artist, scientist, entrepreneur, healthcare professional, or community leader, the knowledge you have gained in this book will help you understand one of the most influential technologies of the twenty-first century. The future of artificial intelligence is still being written, and one day, you may help write the next chapter.

Thank you for taking this journey through the AI Sensor Ecosystem. I hope this book has helped you see that artificial intelligence is not just about machines—it is about people, discovery, responsibility, and the endless possibilities created when knowledge is used to improve the world.

The future is not something we simply inherit—it is something we build together.

Learn AI. Understand AI. Shape the Future.

— Susie Hala
IntelliGloss Press

Chapter 16 Summary

Chapter 16 brought together everything learned throughout this book by showing how artificial intelligence has evolved into one of the most important technologies shaping our world. Students reviewed how AI gathers information through sensors, processes data, makes decisions, performs actions using actuators, and continuously improves through learning and feedback. These individual technologies work together to create intelligent systems that can assist people in solving complex real-world problems.

The chapter emphasized that artificial intelligence begins with information. Cameras, microphones, motion sensors, GPS, satellites, lidar, radar, thermal imaging, and many other technologies provide AI with the information it needs to understand its environment. Artificial intelligence then combines these data sources through sensor fusion, analyzes patterns, makes predictions, and supports decision-making in fields such as healthcare, education, transportation, agriculture, manufacturing, scientific research, and environmental protection.

Students also learned that although AI is becoming increasingly capable, technology alone cannot solve every problem. Human qualities such as creativity, empathy, ethical reasoning, leadership, curiosity, and responsibility remain essential. Artificial intelligence is most effective when it works alongside people rather than replacing them.

The chapter introduced the importance of **ethical AI**, emphasizing fairness, transparency, accountability, privacy, cybersecurity, and responsible innovation. Students discovered that governments, engineers, educators, businesses, families, and citizens all share responsibility for ensuring that AI is developed and used in ways that benefit society.

Finally, the chapter encouraged students to view themselves as the next generation of innovators, problem-solvers, and leaders. Regardless of their future careers, understanding artificial intelligence will help them make informed decisions and participate responsibly in a rapidly changing technological world. The future of AI will ultimately be shaped not only by technology but by the values, character, and wisdom of the people who build and use it.

Reflection

Artificial intelligence is changing the world, but people remain at the center of that change. Throughout this book, you have learned that AI depends on sensors, data, learning, and decision-making. However, the most important lesson is that technology should always serve humanity.

The future will require people who understand not only how AI works but also how to use it responsibly. Engineers will design intelligent systems, teachers will prepare students for new careers, doctors will use AI to improve healthcare, scientists will make new discoveries, and community leaders will help develop policies that protect society while encouraging innovation.

Every generation has been shaped by important technologies. Your generation will help shape the future of artificial intelligence. By continuing to learn, ask questions, think critically, and act responsibly, you can help ensure that AI becomes a force for solving problems, improving lives, and creating opportunities for people around the world.

Student Worksheet

Name: ____

Part A – Vocabulary

Define each term using your own words.

1. Artificial Intelligence

____

____

2. Ethical AI

____

____

3. Innovation

____

____

4. Responsibility

____

____

5. Collaboration

____

____

____

Part B – Short Answer

1. Why is artificial intelligence considered one of the most important technologies of the twenty-first century?

2. Explain why human intelligence and artificial intelligence work best together.

3. List four industries that are being transformed by AI.

4. Why is ethical AI important?

5. How can students prepare themselves for an AI-driven future?

Part C – Critical Thinking

Imagine that you are speaking to a group of younger students about artificial intelligence.

Write one paragraph explaining:

- What AI is.
- Why learning about AI is important.
- How AI can improve people's lives.
- Why humans must continue guiding AI responsibly.

Chapter 16 Quiz

Multiple Choice

1. What is one of the main messages of this chapter?

A. AI will replace all people.

B. AI and humans work best together.

C. AI no longer needs people.

D. AI can solve every problem by itself.

2. Why is ethical AI important?

A. It helps ensure AI is fair, safe, transparent, and responsible.

B. It makes computers run faster.

C. It increases internet speed.

D. It reduces electricity use.

3. Which human quality is difficult for today's AI to fully replicate?

A. Processing large amounts of data

B. Empathy

C. Mathematical calculations

D. Pattern recognition

4. Which of the following industries benefits from AI?

A. Healthcare

B. Education

C. Agriculture

D. All of the above

5. Who will help shape the future of artificial intelligence?

A. Only scientists

B. Only engineers

C. Students, educators, engineers, businesses, governments, and communities working together

D. Only computers

True or False

6. _____ Artificial intelligence depends on information collected from sensors.

7. _____ Human creativity and ethical reasoning remain valuable in the age of AI.

8. _____ Responsible AI development requires human oversight.

9. _____ Understanding AI will become valuable in many different careers.

10. _____ The future of AI depends only on faster computers.

Answer Key

Multiple Choice

1. **B** — AI and humans work best together.
2. **A** — It helps ensure AI is fair, safe, transparent, and responsible.
3. **B** — Empathy
4. **D** — All of the above
5. **C** — Students, educators, engineers, businesses, governments, and communities working together

True or False

6. **True**
7. **True**
8. **True**
9. **True**
10. **False**

Bonus Question

Think about everything you learned throughout this book.

Describe the complete AI cycle—from collecting information to improving through experience—and explain why each step is important.

Sample Answer:

Artificial intelligence begins by collecting information through sensors such as cameras, microphones, GPS, lidar, radar, and motion sensors. It processes and organizes this information, recognizes patterns, and combines data using sensor fusion. AI then evaluates possible actions, makes decisions, and uses actuators to perform physical tasks. After acting, AI receives feedback, learns from the results, and improves future performance. Each step is important because together they allow intelligent systems to observe the world, solve problems, adapt to new situations, and assist people in many areas of daily life.

Classroom Discussion

1. Looking back at this book, what surprised you most about how artificial intelligence works?
2. Why is it important to understand both the strengths and limitations of AI?
3. How can AI improve healthcare, education, transportation, agriculture, and environmental protection while still keeping humans responsible for important decisions?
4. What responsibilities do future engineers, scientists, educators, business leaders, and governments have when developing AI technologies?
5. Imagine yourself 20 years from now. How do you think AI will be part of your career, your community, and your everyday life? How can you help ensure it is used wisely and ethically?

Final Key Takeaways

After completing this book, you should be able to:

- Explain how artificial intelligence uses sensors to observe and understand the world.

- Describe how AI processes information, recognizes patterns, makes decisions, performs actions, and improves through feedback.
- Understand the roles of sensor fusion, actuators, and machine learning in intelligent systems.
- Identify real-world applications of AI in healthcare, education, agriculture, transportation, manufacturing, environmental science, and many other fields.
- Recognize the importance of ethical AI, privacy, cybersecurity, fairness, transparency, and human oversight.
- Compare the strengths of artificial intelligence with the unique qualities of human intelligence.
- Appreciate that the future of AI depends on knowledgeable, responsible people who use technology to improve lives and solve meaningful problems.

Congratulations!

You have completed **The AI Sensor Ecosystem**.

You have explored how artificial intelligence **senses, learns, thinks, decides, acts, and improves**. More importantly, you have learned that AI is not just about technology—it is about people, responsibility, creativity, and using knowledge to build a better future.

This book is only the beginning of your journey. Continue asking questions. Continue learning. Continue exploring. The future of artificial intelligence is still being written, and you have the opportunity to help shape it.

Learn AI. Understand AI. Shape the Future.

— Susie Hala
IntelliGloss Press

AI Glossary —

Letter A

Activation Function

A key part of neural networks that decides whether a neuron should be "activated" or not. It helps the network handle complex patterns, turning raw numbers into meaningful signals during learning.

Algorithm

A step-by-step set of instructions that tells a computer how to solve a problem or perform a task. In AI, algorithms are the "recipes" that guide machines in recognizing patterns, learning from data, and making predictions.

Anomaly Detection

A technique used in AI to find unusual patterns or behaviors that don't fit expected data. It's commonly used in fraud detection, cybersecurity, and system monitoring to identify potential problems

Artificial Intelligence (AI)

The science of creating machines that can perform tasks that normally require human intelligence — such as understanding language, recognizing images, solving problems, or making decisions.

Artificial Neural Network (ANN)

A system inspired by how the human brain works, made up of layers of connected nodes (neurons). Each node processes information and passes it along, allowing the system to "learn" patterns from data.

Artificial General Intelligence (AGI)

A theoretical form of AI that would be able to understand, learn, and perform any intellectual task a human can do. AGI doesn't exist yet, but it represents the ultimate goal of AI research — true human-like intelligence.

Artificial Narrow Intelligence (ANI)

AI designed for a specific task, such as language translation, facial recognition, or driving a car. Most AI today is narrow — powerful at one thing, but unable to perform unrelated tasks.

Attention Mechanism

A method used in advanced AI models (like transformers) that allows the system to focus on the most relevant parts of the input. It helps the AI "pay attention" to important words or data points when generating responses.

Augmented Intelligence

AI systems designed not to replace humans, but to assist them. Augmented intelligence emphasizes collaboration — combining human creativity and judgment with machine speed and accuracy.

Autonomous System

A system that can operate, make decisions, or take actions without direct human control. Examples include self-driving cars, delivery drones, or robotic assistants that use AI to navigate and respond to their environment.

Letter B

Backpropagation

A key learning process used in neural networks to adjust the model's internal settings (weights) based on the errors it makes. By "propagating" mistakes backward through the network, the AI learns to improve accuracy over time.

Batch Learning

A method where an AI model is trained on a complete dataset all at once, rather than learning continuously. It's efficient for large, static datasets but less adaptable to changing data over time.

Bayesian Network

A graphical model that represents the relationships between variables and their probabilities. It helps AI systems reason under uncertainty — for example, predicting the likelihood of an event based on known factors.

Behavioral Analytics

AI techniques that analyze user actions, preferences, or digital patterns to predict future behavior. Often used in marketing, fraud detection, and personalized recommendations.

Bias in AI

When an AI system produces unfair or unbalanced results due to biased data or flawed training methods. Bias can affect hiring systems, loan approvals, and facial recognition — making fairness testing essential in AI development.

Big Data

Extremely large and complex datasets that traditional computers can't easily process. AI tools use big data to learn patterns, make predictions, and uncover insights across industries like healthcare, finance, and marketing.

Binary Classification

A machine learning task where the AI must choose between two possible outcomes — such as "spam or not spam," "yes or no," or "disease or no disease." It's one of the most basic types of AI decision-making.

Bit

The smallest unit of digital data, representing a value of **0** or **1**. In AI and computing, bits form the foundation for all data processing, storage, and communication. Eight bits make up one **byte**, and together they represent everything from numbers and text to images and videos.

Bitwise Operation

A type of mathematical operation that works directly on the binary representation (bits) of data. Bitwise operators (such as AND, OR, XOR, and NOT) are used in AI programming to control low-level logic, optimize performance, and manipulate data efficiently.

Blockchain AI

The combination of blockchain (a secure, distributed ledger) and artificial intelligence to improve transparency, data security, and trust in AI-driven systems.

Bot

Short for "robot," a bot is a program that performs automated tasks. In AI, chatbots are designed to simulate human conversation, while other bots perform repetitive digital actions like data scraping or scheduling.

Brute Force Algorithm

A simple but computationally expensive problem-solving method that tries every possible solution until it finds the correct one. Though inefficient, it guarantees accuracy for small problems.

AI Glossary — Letter C

Chatbot

An AI-powered program designed to simulate human conversation through text or voice. Chatbots can answer questions, provide customer support, teach lessons, or help automate business communication using natural language processing.

Classification

A core machine learning task where AI assigns input data into specific categories or labels — such as identifying whether an email is "spam" or "not spam." Classification models are trained using labeled examples to recognize patterns.

Clustering

An unsupervised learning technique where AI groups similar pieces of data together based on shared characteristics. Unlike classification, clustering doesn't use labeled data — it helps uncover hidden patterns or natural groupings within datasets.

Cognitive Computing

A branch of AI that mimics human reasoning, perception, and decision-making. Cognitive systems analyze unstructured data, recognize language and emotions, and provide intelligent suggestions — much like how the human brain interprets information.

Computer Vision

A field of AI that enables machines to "see" and interpret visual information such as images or videos. Computer vision powers facial recognition, object detection, medical imaging, and autonomous vehicles.

Convolutional Neural Network (CNN)

A specialized type of neural network used primarily for image and video analysis. CNNs automatically detect visual features like edges, shapes, and textures, allowing machines to recognize objects or patterns with high accuracy.

Context Window

The range of text or tokens that a language model can "see" and use at one time to generate its response. A larger context window allows AI to remember more of the conversation, leading to better understanding and consistency.

Corpus

A large and structured collection of texts used to train or evaluate language models. In AI, a corpus provides the examples that teach the model how words and phrases are used in real-world contexts.

Cross-Validation

A model evaluation technique used in machine learning to test how well a model generalizes to new, unseen data. The dataset is divided into parts (folds), and the model is trained and tested multiple times to ensure accuracy and reliability.

Cybernetics

The interdisciplinary study of communication and control in both machines and living organisms. In AI, cybernetics explores feedback loops — how systems monitor and adjust their behavior to maintain balance and achieve goals.

Letter D

Data Analytics

The process of examining, cleaning, and interpreting data to uncover useful information and patterns. In AI, data analytics helps models learn from real-world data to make predictions and informed decisions.

Data Labeling

The act of tagging or annotating raw data with meaningful labels — such as identifying images with "cat" or "dog." Labeled data is essential for training supervised machine learning models.

Data Mining

The practice of exploring large datasets to discover hidden patterns, trends, or relationships. AI-powered data mining helps businesses predict customer behavior, detect fraud, and improve decision-making.

Data Science

An interdisciplinary field that combines statistics, programming, and AI to extract insights from data. Data scientists build predictive models, analyze trends, and guide data-driven decisions.

Dataset

A structured collection of data used to train or test AI models. A dataset can include text, images, numbers, or audio. The quality and diversity of the dataset directly affect how well an AI performs.

Decision Tree

A visual and logical model used in AI for decision-making. Each branch represents a question or condition, and each leaf represents an outcome. Decision trees are popular for their simplicity and interpretability.

Deep Learning

A subset of machine learning that uses multi-layered neural networks to learn complex patterns. Deep learning powers technologies like voice recognition, autonomous driving, and image generation.

Dimensionality Reduction

A mathematical process used to simplify datasets by reducing the number of variables while preserving important information. It helps AI models work faster and more efficiently, especially with large data.

Domain Adaptation

A technique in AI that allows a model trained on one dataset to perform well on a different but related dataset. It helps AI generalize better to new environments or data types.

Drift Detection

The process of identifying when an AI model's performance declines because real-world data has changed. Detecting data drift ensures the model stays accurate and up-to-date over time.

Letter E

E-book Recommendation Systems

AI algorithms that suggest books or reading materials based on user preferences, past selections, or browsing behavior. They enhance reading platforms by delivering personalized content to readers.

E-Brainstorming

The use of AI tools to assist with creative idea generation. E-brainstorming platforms help individuals and teams generate fresh perspectives, organize thoughts, and develop new solutions quickly.

E-commerce AI

AI applications that enhance online shopping experiences. These systems recommend products, predict customer behavior, optimize pricing, and improve inventory management for e-commerce platforms.

Edge AI

Artificial Intelligence that runs directly on local devices (like smartphones, cameras, or IoT sensors) instead of relying on cloud servers. Edge AI allows faster responses, improved privacy, and reduced internet dependency.

E-Learning AI

The use of AI in online education to personalize learning experiences, analyze student performance, and recommend tailored study materials. E-Learning AI helps teachers and learners adapt lessons to individual needs.

E-mail Filtering AI

AI systems that automatically detect and organize incoming emails — such as sorting spam, prioritizing important messages, or detecting phishing threats — using natural language and pattern recognition.

Embedding

A mathematical representation of data (like words, sentences, or images) in numerical form. In AI, embeddings help models understand meaning, context, and similarity — crucial for natural language processing and image recognition.

Emotion AI

Also called Affective Computing, it's a branch of AI that recognizes, interprets, and responds to human emotions using facial expressions, voice tones, or physiological signals. It's used in customer service, education, and healthcare.

Ensemble Learning

A technique that combines multiple AI models to produce stronger, more accurate results than a single model could achieve alone. Common ensemble methods include bagging, boosting, and stacking.

E-Transaction Security

AI-based systems that monitor and protect online financial transactions. They detect unusual activity, verify identities, and prevent fraud in digital banking and online payment systems.

Letter F

Face Recognition AI

A technology that uses machine learning and computer vision to identify or verify a person's identity based on facial features. It's used in security systems, smartphones, and law enforcement, but also raises privacy and ethical concerns.

False Positive

A situation in which an AI system incorrectly identifies something as true when it's not. For example, a spam filter marking a legitimate email as spam. Reducing false positives improves reliability and user trust.

False Negative

The opposite of a false positive — when an AI system fails to identify something that is true. For example, a medical AI missing signs of a disease. Balancing false positives and negatives is vital in sensitive applications.

Feature Engineering

The process of creating, transforming, or selecting data features to improve machine learning model performance. It's a key step that combines human insight with data science techniques to optimize accuracy.

Feature Extraction

The process of identifying the most important characteristics or variables from raw data. In AI, feature extraction helps reduce complexity and improve model accuracy by focusing on relevant information.

Feature Map

In deep learning, particularly in convolutional neural networks (CNNs), a feature map represents visual patterns detected in an image. It helps the network recognize shapes, textures, and other important details.

Federated Learning

A training method that allows multiple devices or organizations to collaboratively train an AI model without sharing raw data. Each participant trains the model locally, and only updates are shared — improving data privacy and security.

Fine-Tuning

A process of retraining a pre-trained AI model on a smaller, specific dataset to make it more accurate for a particular task. Fine-tuning allows developers to customize general-purpose models for specialized applications.

Forecasting Model

An AI system that predicts future events or trends based on historical data. Forecasting models are widely used in business, weather prediction, finance, and supply chain management.

Fuzzy Logic

An AI reasoning system that allows for partial truths rather than strict "true or false" decisions. It's useful for handling uncertainty in real-world situations like temperature control, medical diagnosis, and robotics.

Letter G

GAN (Generative Adversarial Network)

A type of deep learning model with two neural networks — a **generator** and a **discriminator** — that work against each other. The generator creates data (like images or text), while the discriminator evaluates it for authenticity. This competition helps the model generate highly realistic outputs such as AI-generated art or photos.

General AI (Artificial General Intelligence)

A theoretical form of AI capable of understanding, learning, and applying knowledge across multiple domains — much like a human being. Unlike narrow AI, General AI could perform any intellectual task without specific training.

Genetic Algorithm

An optimization technique inspired by natural selection. It uses processes like mutation, crossover, and selection to evolve solutions to complex problems — often used in robotics, scheduling, and engineering design.

Geospatial AI

The combination of artificial intelligence with geographic data (maps, satellite images, or GPS data) to analyze spatial patterns. It's used in urban planning, agriculture, environmental monitoring, and disaster management.

Gesture Recognition

A branch of computer vision that interprets human movements — such as hand waves or facial expressions — as commands. It's commonly used in gaming, virtual reality, and touchless interfaces.

GPT (Generative Pre-trained Transformer)

A family of large language models developed by OpenAI. GPT models are trained on vast text datasets and can generate human-like text, write essays, code, or answer questions — forming the foundation for conversational AI systems like ChatGPT.

Gradient Descent

An optimization algorithm used in training neural networks. It minimizes the model's prediction error by gradually adjusting weights in the direction of the steepest decrease in loss — similar to rolling downhill to find the lowest point.

Graph Neural Network (GNN)

A type of neural network designed to process data structured as graphs — with nodes (points) and edges (connections). GNNs are used in recommendation systems, molecule analysis, and social network modeling.

Ground Truth

The real, verified data used to measure how accurate an AI model's predictions are. For example, in image recognition, the "ground truth" is the actual label of what the image shows. It's essential for evaluating model performance.

Guided Learning

An AI-assisted educational approach that provides learners with personalized hints, explanations, and progress tracking. Guided learning uses data analytics and adaptive models to support student growth in real time.

Letter H

Hallucination (in AI)

A phenomenon where an AI model generates information that appears confident and factual but is actually incorrect or fabricated. Hallucinations occur when the model fills gaps in knowledge or misinterprets data. Managing them requires clear prompts, human review, and fact-checking.

Heuristic Algorithm

A problem-solving method that uses experience-based shortcuts to find good — though not always perfect — solutions quickly. Heuristic algorithms are common in AI search systems, decision-making, and optimization problems where speed matters more than precision.

Hidden Layer

A layer of neurons in a neural network that processes inputs between the input and output layers. Hidden layers extract complex patterns from data and enable the network to make accurate predictions or classifications.

Human-Computer Interaction (HCI)

The study and design of how people interact with computers and AI systems. HCI focuses on usability, accessibility, and user experience, ensuring that AI tools feel intuitive and supportive to human users.

Human-in-the-Loop (HITL)

An AI training or decision process that includes active human participation. Humans review, correct, or guide the AI's outputs to ensure quality, fairness, and ethical alignment — especially important in high-stakes fields like healthcare and law.

Hybrid AI

An approach that combines two or more types of AI — such as symbolic reasoning (rule-based) and machine learning (data-driven) — to create systems that are both interpretable and powerful. Hybrid AI blends logic with learning for smarter, explainable outcomes.

Hyperparameter

A setting or configuration that controls how an AI model learns, such as learning rate, batch size, or number of layers. Unlike model parameters learned automatically, hyperparameters are manually chosen to optimize training performance.

Hyperparameter Tuning

The process of finding the best hyperparameter values for a model. It's often done through techniques like grid search, random search, or Bayesian optimization to achieve the highest accuracy possible.

Hypothesis Testing (in AI)

A statistical method for evaluating whether a pattern or relationship found by an AI model is real or due to chance. It helps ensure that model results are meaningful and scientifically valid.

Hybrid Cloud AI

A cloud computing setup that uses both private and public cloud environments to train and deploy AI models. It offers flexibility, scalability, and stronger control over sensitive data.

Letter I

Image Recognition

A branch of computer vision that enables AI systems to identify and categorize objects, people, or scenes in images. It's used in facial recognition, medical imaging, self-driving cars, and quality control in manufacturing.

Imbalanced Data

A situation where some classes or categories in a dataset have many more examples than others. Imbalanced data can cause AI models to favor the majority class, leading to inaccurate predictions. Balancing data improves fairness and performance.

Inference Engine

A component of an AI system that applies logical rules or learned patterns to reach conclusions or make decisions. Inference engines are core parts of expert systems and modern language models that generate intelligent responses.

Information Retrieval

The process of searching, extracting, and ranking relevant data from large datasets or documents. AI-powered search engines and chatbots use information retrieval to deliver accurate, context-aware answers.

Input Data

The raw information — such as text, numbers, or images — that an AI system receives before processing. The quality of input data directly affects the reliability of the model's output.

Intelligent Agent

A software entity capable of perceiving its environment, making decisions, and taking actions to achieve specific goals. Examples include virtual assistants, recommendation systems, and AI tutors.

Interpretable AI

An approach to AI design focused on making model decisions understandable to humans. Interpretable AI helps users trust and verify machine-generated outcomes, especially in healthcare, finance, and law.

Iterative Learning

A process where an AI model improves through repeated cycles of training, testing, and refining. Each iteration helps the system learn from its mistakes and perform better over time.

IoT (Internet of Things) AI

AI integrated with smart devices connected through the internet. IoT AI enables objects like thermostats, watches, and appliances to learn user preferences, predict behavior, and operate autonomously.

Isolation Forest

An anomaly detection algorithm that identifies unusual data points by isolating them from the rest of the dataset. It's efficient for spotting fraud, system errors, or rare events.

Letter J

Jaccard Index

A statistical measure used to compare the similarity between two sets. In AI and machine learning, it's often used to evaluate clustering or text similarity by dividing the intersection of sets by their union.

Java (in AI)

A programming language often used in AI applications due to its portability, scalability, and strong memory management. Java supports frameworks like Deeplearning4j and Weka, which help in building AI systems for enterprise and academic use.

Joint Embedding

A technique where two or more types of data — such as text and images — are represented in a shared vector space. Joint embeddings allow AI to link visual and textual understanding, as seen in models like CLIP that connect words to images.

JSON (JavaScript Object Notation)

A lightweight data format used for storing and exchanging structured information between systems. AI tools often use JSON to send model inputs, outputs, and metadata in a clear and readable way.

Jump Learning

An advanced learning concept where AI "jumps ahead" in reasoning or skill based on prior knowledge, instead of learning everything from scratch. It mimics human intuition and helps reduce training time in complex models.

Letter K

Keyword Extraction

A natural language processing technique used to identify the most relevant words or phrases within text. It helps summarize content, improve search results, and enhance AI-driven document classification.

Kernel Function

A mathematical function used in Support Vector Machines (SVMs) to transform data into a higher-dimensional space. This allows the AI to separate complex, non-linear data more effectively. Common kernel types include linear, polynomial, and radial basis functions.

Kinetic AI

A branch of AI that studies movement and motion analysis. It's used in robotics, sports technology, and autonomous vehicles to understand physical actions and predict motion patterns.

K-Means Clustering

An unsupervised learning algorithm that divides data into *K* distinct groups based on similarity. It assigns each data point to the cluster with the nearest mean value. K-Means is widely used in customer segmentation, image compression, and pattern recognition.

K-Nearest Neighbor (KNN)

A simple yet powerful machine learning algorithm that classifies data based on its proximity to *K* neighboring points. It assumes similar data points are likely to have similar outcomes. KNN is used in recommendation systems and predictive analytics.

Knowledge Base

A structured collection of information that an AI system uses to answer questions, make decisions, or provide explanations. Knowledge bases power systems like virtual assistants, expert systems, and search engines.

Knowledge Distillation

A process where a smaller AI model learns from a larger, more complex model. This helps create faster, lightweight systems that maintain strong performance while using fewer computational resources.

Knowledge Graph

A network that connects information through relationships and context, enabling AI systems to understand how data points relate. Knowledge graphs are used by companies like Google to enhance search accuracy and context understanding.

Knowledge Representation

The method of encoding information in a way that AI systems can understand and use for reasoning. It includes logic rules, ontologies, and semantic networks, allowing AI to store and apply knowledge intelligently.

Knowledge Transfer

A technique in AI and machine learning where knowledge gained from one task or dataset is reused in another. This reduces the need for retraining from scratch and speeds up learning in related areas.

Letter L

Label Encoding

A data preprocessing technique used to convert categorical (text-based) values into numerical form so that AI models can process them. For example, "Red," "Green," and "Blue" may be encoded as 0, 1, and 2.

Labeled Data

Data that has been tagged with correct answers or classifications, such as images labeled "cat" or "dog." Labeled data is essential for training supervised learning models that rely on known outcomes.

Language Model

An AI system trained to understand, predict, and generate human language. It learns from massive text datasets to perform tasks like translation, summarization, and conversation — examples include GPT and Gemini.

Latent Space

A hidden mathematical representation within an AI model that captures complex relationships between data points. In generative AI, latent space allows systems to create new images, sounds, or text by exploring abstract features.

Lazy Learning

A machine learning approach where the model delays generalization until a prediction is requested. Algorithms like K-Nearest Neighbor (KNN) store data and only compute results when needed, trading speed for flexibility.

Linear Regression

A basic yet powerful algorithm that predicts outcomes by finding the best-fitting straight line through data points. It's commonly used in finance, sales forecasting, and scientific analysis.

Logistic Regression

A classification algorithm used to predict categorical outcomes (like "yes" or "no") instead of continuous values. Despite its name, it's mainly used for probability-based classification rather than regression.

Long Short-Term Memory (LSTM)

A special type of recurrent neural network (RNN) designed to remember long-term dependencies in sequential data, such as language or time series. LSTMs are used in speech recognition, translation, and text generation.

Loss Function

A mathematical formula that measures how far an AI model's predictions are from the correct answers. The goal of training is to minimize this loss, helping the model improve accuracy over time.

Low-Code AI

AI tools that allow users to build and deploy machine learning models with minimal coding. They simplify development for non-programmers, empowering educators, entrepreneurs, and small businesses to use AI effectively.

Letter M

Machine Learning (ML)

A core branch of AI where systems learn from data to make predictions or decisions without being explicitly programmed. It powers tools like recommendation engines, fraud detection, and voice recognition.

Meta Learning

Also called "learning to learn," this technique trains AI systems to adapt quickly to new tasks by using prior knowledge. Meta learning helps models generalize better with less training data.

Model Training

The process of teaching an AI model to recognize patterns by feeding it large amounts of data. During training, the model adjusts its internal parameters to minimize errors and improve predictions.

Model Evaluation

A step where an AI model's accuracy and performance are tested using data it hasn't seen before. Evaluation ensures that the model works well in real-world scenarios.

Model Overfitting

A situation where an AI model learns too closely from training data, capturing noise instead of patterns. Overfitting causes poor performance on new data. Regularization and validation help prevent it.

Model Optimization

The process of improving an AI model's efficiency, accuracy, and speed by fine-tuning its architecture, parameters, or algorithms.

Monte Carlo Simulation

A statistical method that uses random sampling to estimate outcomes in uncertain situations. AI systems use it for risk analysis, forecasting, and game simulations.

Multimodal AI

An AI system capable of understanding and processing information from multiple sources — such as text, images, sound, and video — to produce richer and more accurate results.

Multi-Agent System

A group of AI agents that work together or compete to achieve individual or shared goals. They are used in simulations, logistics, and automated trading systems.

Mutation Algorithm

A process inspired by genetics where random changes are introduced to improve AI models' performance during optimization or evolutionary learning.

Letter N

Naive Bayes Algorithm

A simple but powerful machine learning algorithm based on probability. It's widely used in spam detection, text classification, and sentiment analysis.

Named Entity Recognition (NER)

An NLP technique that identifies and classifies specific names or entities (like people, places, or organizations) within text.

Natural Language Processing (NLP)

A field of AI that enables machines to understand and respond to human language. It powers chatbots, translation tools, and voice assistants.

Natural Language Understanding (NLU)

A subset of NLP that focuses on interpreting meaning, emotion, and intent behind text or speech. It allows AI to understand context and tone.

Neural Architecture Search (NAS)

An automated method for designing neural networks. AI systems use NAS to discover optimal model structures without human intervention.

Neural Network

A computational model inspired by the human brain, made of layers of nodes (neurons) that process data. Neural networks are the foundation of deep learning systems.

Neuron

Definition

In artificial intelligence and machine learning, a **neuron** (also called a *node* or *unit*) is the fundamental building block of an artificial neural network. It is modeled loosely after the biological neuron found in the human brain. Each artificial neuron receives input signals, processes them mathematically, and produces an output that is passed to other neurons in the network. Neurons collectively enable a model to learn, recognize patterns, and make predictions by adjusting their internal parameters during training.

Key Components

1. **Inputs:**
   The data values or signals that are fed into the neuron — similar to how biological neurons receive signals through dendrites.
2. **Weights:**
   Numerical values assigned to each input that determine their importance. The neuron learns by adjusting these weights during training.
3. **Summation Function:**
   A mathematical operation that combines the weighted inputs into a single value, often using a simple addition or dot product.
4. **Activation Function:**
   A non-linear function (such as ReLU, Sigmoid, or Tanh) applied to the summation result to decide whether the neuron should "fire" or remain inactive.
5. **Output:**
   The final result produced by the neuron after applying the activation function, which becomes the input for other neurons in subsequent layers.

Benefits

- Allows complex relationships to be learned from raw data.
- Enables non-linear transformations for deep learning tasks.
- Builds scalable and flexible structures that can adapt to various problems.
- Mimics the way biological neurons communicate and adapt over time.

Disadvantages

- Individual neurons are simple and limited in function; meaningful behavior arises only when many are connected.
- May become computationally expensive as the network grows deeper.
- Can overfit data if not properly regularized.

Examples

- A neuron in a **convolutional neural network (CNN)** may detect visual patterns such as edges or textures.
- In a **language model**, neurons may learn linguistic features like word order or meaning.
- In **speech recognition**, neurons can capture tone, pitch, and pronunciation patterns.

Applications

- **Image Recognition:** Detecting and classifying objects, faces, or handwriting.
- **Natural Language Processing:** Understanding text, context, and sentiment.
- **Financial Forecasting:** Identifying market trends from numerical data.
- **Medical Diagnosis:** Interpreting scans, patterns, and patient records.

Industries Using Neuron-Based Models

- **Healthcare:** Predictive diagnosis and imaging analysis.
- **Education:** Adaptive learning and student performance prediction.
- **Technology:** AI assistants, chatbots, and autonomous systems.
- **Transportation:** Self-driving cars and sensor-based navigation.

Challenges

- Understanding neuron-level decision-making remains difficult, leading to "black box" behavior.
- Requires large amounts of data and computational resources to train effectively.
- Sensitive to data quality — poor input can lead to unreliable neuron activation.

Summary

A **neuron** is the core unit of intelligence within an artificial neural network. By processing inputs through weighted connections and activation functions, neurons enable machines to simulate learning and reasoning similar to the human brain. Though individually simple, millions of interconnected neurons together form the foundation of modern AI systems, powering technologies from image recognition to natural language understanding.

Node

A basic unit in a neural network that receives input, processes it, and sends it forward. Nodes collectively form layers that learn from data.

Noise (in Data)

Random or irrelevant information in a dataset that can confuse AI models. Removing noise improves accuracy and training efficiency.

Nonlinear Activation

A mathematical function in neural networks that allows models to learn complex, non-straight-line relationships. Common examples include ReLU, Sigmoid, and Tanh functions.

Normalization

A data preprocessing step that scales values into a consistent range to help AI models learn faster and perform better.

Letter O

Object Detection

A computer vision technique that identifies and locates objects within an image or video. It's used in autonomous driving, security systems, and retail analytics.

Objective Function

A mathematical formula that defines the goal of an AI model — usually to minimize error or maximize accuracy. It guides the learning process during training.

One-Hot Encoding

A method used to represent categorical data numerically by converting each value into a binary vector. It helps AI systems interpret text-based or labeled inputs.

Ontology (in AI)

A structured framework that defines relationships between concepts within a domain. Ontologies help AI organize knowledge logically and reason effectively.

Optimization Algorithm

A method used to adjust model parameters during training to minimize loss and improve accuracy. Examples include Gradient Descent and Adam Optimizer.

Optimization Problem

A task in AI where the goal is to find the best possible solution — like minimizing cost or maximizing performance — under certain constraints.

Outlier Detection

The process of identifying data points that deviate significantly from the rest. Outlier detection helps find errors, fraud, or anomalies.

Overfitting

When an AI model performs well on training data but fails to generalize to new data because it memorized instead of learning patterns.

Overparameterization

A condition where an AI model has more parameters than necessary, often leading to overfitting and inefficiency.

Oversampling

A data balancing technique that increases the number of examples in an underrepresented class to prevent bias during training.

Letter P

Parameter

A value inside an AI model that determines how it makes predictions. Parameters are adjusted during training to minimize error and improve accuracy.

Pattern Recognition

The ability of AI systems to identify regularities, trends, or structures in data. It's used in handwriting recognition, medical imaging, and speech analysis.

Perceptron

One of the earliest types of artificial neural networks. It consists of a single layer of nodes and is used for simple classification tasks.

Predictive Analytics

A branch of AI that uses statistical models and machine learning to forecast future events based on historical data.

Preprocessing

The preparation of data before feeding it into an AI model — including cleaning, scaling, and encoding — to ensure accuracy and consistency.

Probability Distribution

A statistical function that describes the likelihood of different outcomes in a dataset. It's essential for probabilistic reasoning and uncertainty modeling in AI.

Prompt Engineering

The practice of crafting precise and intentional instructions (prompts) to guide AI models in generating accurate and creative responses. It's the foundation of effective human-AI communication.

Probability Distribution

A statistical function that describes the likelihood of different outcomes in a dataset. It's essential for probabilistic reasoning and uncertainty modeling in AI.

Python (Programming Language)

A versatile, easy-to-learn programming language widely used in AI and data science. Python supports major libraries like TensorFlow, PyTorch, and Scikit-learn, making it the most popular tool for AI development.

Pre-trained Model

An AI model that has already been trained on large datasets and can be fine-tuned for specific tasks. Using pre-trained models saves time and computing resources.

Precision and Recall

Two key metrics for evaluating AI performance. **Precision** measures accuracy among positive predictions, while **Recall** measures how many actual positives were correctly identified.

Letter Q

Q-Learning

A type of reinforcement learning algorithm where an agent learns to make decisions by receiving rewards or penalties. It helps AI systems determine the best action to take in each situation, such as in robotics or game AI.

Quantization

A technique that reduces the precision of numbers in AI models to make them smaller and faster without major loss in accuracy. It's commonly used to optimize models for mobile or edge devices.

Quantum AI

The integration of quantum computing and artificial intelligence. Quantum AI uses the principles of quantum mechanics to process complex computations faster than traditional computers.

Query

A request for information sent to a database or AI system. In natural language models, queries are user inputs — the "questions" that trigger responses.

Queue Learning

A data-handling strategy where information is processed sequentially, one at a time. It's useful for managing AI tasks or workflows that must follow a specific order.

Letter R

Random Forest

An ensemble learning algorithm that combines multiple decision trees to improve accuracy and reduce overfitting. It's used for both classification and regression tasks.

Recurrent Neural Network (RNN)

A neural network designed for sequential data such as text, speech, or time series. RNNs have loops that allow them to "remember" previous inputs, making them ideal for language and forecasting tasks.

Regression Analysis

A statistical method that models the relationship between variables to predict future outcomes. Linear and logistic regression are common types.

Reinforcement Learning

An AI learning method where an agent interacts with its environment and learns from feedback through rewards and penalties. It's used in robotics, gaming, and automation.

Representation Learning

A machine learning technique where the system automatically discovers useful features from raw data instead of relying on manual feature selection.

Retrieval-Augmented Generation (RAG)

A model that combines information retrieval and text generation. It fetches relevant data before producing a response, improving accuracy in AI question-answering systems.

Reward Function

A key component of reinforcement learning that defines how much "reward" an AI receives for taking certain actions. It guides the system toward desirable outcomes.

Robotic Process Automation (RPA)

Technology that uses AI to automate repetitive digital tasks, such as data entry or document processing, to increase efficiency and reduce human error.

Rule-Based System

An AI system that makes decisions based on predefined rules or conditions, often used in expert systems or early AI programs.

Runtime Environment

The system or platform where AI models are executed. It includes the software, hardware, and configurations required for the model to function properly.

Letter S

Scalability

The ability of an AI system to handle increasing amounts of data or users without losing performance. Scalable AI models grow with business and computational needs.

Semi-Supervised Learning

A learning method that combines a small amount of labeled data with a large amount of unlabeled data to improve model performance.

Sentiment Analysis

A natural language processing technique that identifies emotions or opinions in text, such as positive, negative, or neutral sentiment. It's used in marketing and social media monitoring.

Signal Processing

The analysis and transformation of data signals (like sound, images, or time series) into meaningful patterns. AI uses it in speech recognition and medical imaging.

Speech Recognition

A technology that converts spoken language into text using AI models trained on voice data. It powers virtual assistants and transcription tools.

Supervised Learning

A machine learning technique where a model is trained using labeled data, meaning both inputs and correct outputs are provided during training.

Swarm Intelligence

An AI concept inspired by nature, where simple agents (like ants or bees) collectively solve complex problems. It's used in optimization, robotics, and network routing.

8. Symbolic AI

An early AI approach based on logical rules and symbolic representations. Unlike modern machine learning, it uses explicit reasoning rather than pattern recognition.

Synthetic Data

Artificially generated data created to train AI models when real data is limited or sensitive. It helps improve privacy and expand datasets.

Letter T

Target Variable

The specific outcome or label that an AI model aims to predict, such as "spam or not spam" or "disease present or absent."

TensorFlow

An open-source AI framework developed by Google that helps developers build and train machine learning models efficiently.

Token (Artificial Intelligence)

Definition
A **token** is a small unit of language that artificial intelligence systems use to process, analyze, and generate text. Instead of reading full sentences like humans do, AI models break language into smaller pieces called tokens so that computers can process the information mathematically.

Tokens may represent a whole word, part of a word, a number, punctuation mark, or symbol. Each token is converted into a numerical value that the AI system can analyze during training and prediction.

Example
The sentence:

Artificial intelligence is powerful.

may be broken into tokens such as:

Artificial | intelligence | is | powerful | .

These tokens are then converted into numerical representations that allow the AI model to understand patterns in language.

Role in Artificial Intelligence
Tokens serve two important roles in AI systems:

Language Processing Units – Tokens allow AI models to read and generate human language by breaking text into manageable pieces that can be analyzed mathematically.

Computation Measurement Units – Because AI systems process text token by token, tokens are also used to measure how much computing work a model performs. For this reason, tokens are often described as the "currency" of AI usage.

Applications
Tokens are essential in many artificial intelligence technologies, including:

Natural language processing

Machine translation

AI chatbots

Text generation systems

Speech recognition systems

Document analysis tools

Summary
Tokens are the basic language units that allow artificial intelligence systems to understand and generate human communication. By converting text into tokens, AI models can analyze language patterns and produce meaningful responses.

Token Limit

The maximum number of tokens (words or symbols) an AI model can process in a single interaction or context window

Tokenization

The process of breaking text into smaller units, or "tokens," such as words or subwords, to help AI models understand language.

Transfer Learning

A technique where a model pre-trained on one task is adapted to a different but related task, saving time and improving performance.

Transformer Architecture

Definition

Transformer Architecture is a deep learning model framework introduced in 2017 by Vaswani et al. in the paper *"Attention Is All You Need."* It revolutionized natural language processing (NLP) by replacing traditional sequence models like RNNs (Recurrent Neural Networks) and LSTMs (Long Short-Term Memory networks) with a mechanism known as **self-attention**, allowing the model to understand relationships between words or elements in a sequence — regardless of their distance from each other.

Key Components

1. **Encoder-Decoder Structure:**
   The architecture typically has two main parts — the encoder, which reads and represents the input data, and the decoder, which generates the output based on the encoded information.
2. **Self-Attention Mechanism:**
   This mechanism lets the model weigh the importance of each word relative to others in a sentence, improving context understanding.
3. **Multi-Head Attention:**
   Multiple attention layers run in parallel, enabling the model to capture different kinds of relationships or meanings simultaneously.
4. **Positional Encoding:**
   Since Transformers do not process data sequentially, positional encodings are added to indicate the order of elements in a sentence.
5. **Feed-Forward Networks:**
   After attention layers, fully connected neural networks help the model transform and refine the contextual representations.
6. **Residual Connections and Layer Normalization:**
   These ensure stability during training and help the model learn complex patterns efficiently.

Benefits

- Handles long-range dependencies more effectively than RNNs.
- Enables parallel processing, making it faster to train on large datasets.
- Produces state-of-the-art performance across multiple tasks, such as translation, summarization, and text generation.
- Scales well to massive datasets and larger models like GPT, BERT, and T5.

Disadvantages

- Extremely data- and computation-intensive, requiring powerful hardware.
- Can be prone to bias if trained on unbalanced or low-quality datasets.
- Difficult to interpret because of its complexity and multi-layered attention mechanisms.

Applications

- **Natural Language Processing (NLP):** Machine translation, text summarization, sentiment analysis, and chatbots.
- **Vision Transformers (ViTs):** Image recognition and object detection in computer vision.
- **Speech Recognition:** Improved context-aware transcription and voice command systems.
- **Multimodal AI:** Combining text, images, and audio for generative and reasoning tasks.

Industries Using Transformer Models

- **Technology:** Google, OpenAI, Meta, and Microsoft for large-scale AI systems.
- **Education:** Intelligent tutoring systems and adaptive learning platforms.
- **Healthcare:** Medical data analysis and clinical text interpretation.
- **Entertainment:** Script generation, gaming narratives, and subtitles translation.

Challenges

- High energy consumption during training and inference.
- Potential for producing inaccurate or biased outputs if the model is not fine-tuned properly.
- Data privacy concerns in large-scale, open-domain training environments.

Summary

The Transformer Architecture represents a fundamental shift in how machines understand and generate language. Its self-attention mechanism allows models to process context more globally and flexibly than ever before. Transformers laid the foundation for today's most advanced AI systems — including ChatGPT, BERT, and countless others — marking a turning point in modern artificial intelligence.

Transformer Model

A neural network architecture that processes sequences of data (like text) more efficiently than traditional RNNs. It's the foundation of modern large language models such as GPT.

Training Data

The dataset used to teach an AI model. Training data must be diverse and accurate to ensure reliable model performance.

Turing Test

A test developed by Alan Turing to evaluate whether a machine can exhibit intelligent behavior indistinguishable from that of a human.

Time Series Analysis

The use of AI to analyze sequential data over time, such as stock prices or weather patterns, to forecast future trends.

Tunable Parameters

Adjustable values in an AI model that influence its performance, such as learning rate or layer depth. Tuning helps achieve optimal results.

Letter U

Unlabeled Data

Data that has not been tagged with specific outputs or categories. It's commonly used in unsupervised and semi-supervised learning.

Unstructured Data

Information that doesn't follow a predefined format, such as text, images, videos, or social media posts. AI tools process it using natural language and computer vision techniques.

Unsupervised Learning

A machine learning method where models learn from unlabeled data to find patterns, groupings, or hidden structures without specific instructions.

Uncertainty Modeling

The process of estimating how confident an AI model is about its predictions. It helps improve trust and decision-making in sensitive domains like medicine or finance.

Update Rate

The frequency at which an AI model adjusts its parameters during training. A balanced update rate ensures faster learning without instability.

User Intent Recognition

An NLP technique that determines the purpose or goal behind a user's input — essential in chatbots and voice assistants for accurate responses.

Utility Function

A mathematical function used in AI to evaluate the desirability or usefulness of different actions. It's often used in decision-making and reinforcement learning.

Letter V

Validation Set

A portion of the dataset used during model training to fine-tune parameters and prevent overfitting. It helps evaluate how well the model generalizes to unseen data before final testing.

Value Function (in Reinforcement Learning)

A function that estimates the expected reward an AI agent will receive from a certain state or action. It guides decision-making by helping the agent choose actions that maximize long-term rewards.

Variance (in AI Models)

A measure of how much a model's predictions change when trained on different data samples. High variance means the model is sensitive to noise and may overfit.

Vectorization

The process of converting data (like text or images) into numerical vectors that AI models can process. It's essential in natural language processing and computer vision.

Verification (in AI Systems)

The process of checking whether an AI model or system performs its intended function correctly and safely before deployment.

Virtual Agent

An AI-driven digital assistant designed to interact with humans through voice or text. Examples include chatbots, customer service bots, and AI tutors.

Virtual Reality (VR)

A computer-generated environment that simulates real or imagined worlds. When combined with AI, VR can create adaptive, interactive learning and training experiences.

Vision Transformer (ViT)

A deep learning model that applies transformer architecture — originally used for language — to image recognition tasks. It divides images into patches and processes them like words in a sentence.

Voice Recognition

AI technology that identifies and processes human voices to perform tasks, such as unlocking devices or activating voice assistants.

Volumetric Data

Three-dimensional data used in fields like medical imaging, 3D modeling, and geoscience. AI uses it to analyze structures and visualize depth in complex environments.

Letter W

Weak AI (Narrow AI)

AI designed to perform a specific task, such as translation or image classification. It does not possess general reasoning or consciousness like humans.

Weight (in Neural Networks)

A numerical value that determines the strength of a connection between neurons. During training, weights are adjusted to reduce prediction errors.

Weighted Average

A statistical method that assigns different importance (weights) to data points when calculating an average. AI uses it to prioritize more relevant or reliable data.

Whisper Model

An AI model developed by OpenAI for automatic speech recognition (ASR). It transcribes and translates spoken language into text across multiple languages with high accuracy.

Wi-Fi Sensing AI

Technology that uses Wi-Fi signals to detect movement or monitor environments without cameras. It's used in security, healthcare, and smart homes.

Windowing Function

A mathematical function used in signal processing and speech recognition to divide data into smaller segments for analysis.

Word Embedding

A representation of words in numerical form where similar words are placed close together in vector space. It helps AI models understand semantic relationships in text.

Word2Vec

A popular algorithm for creating word embeddings by learning relationships between words based on their context within large text datasets.

Workflow Automation

The use of AI to streamline repetitive business tasks such as approvals, document sorting, and scheduling. It increases productivity and reduces human error.

World Model (in AI)

A conceptual model an AI system builds to understand and predict the behavior of the environment around it — especially in robotics and autonomous systems.

Letter X

XAI (Explainable AI)

A field of AI focused on making models transparent and understandable to humans. It explains how decisions are made, which builds trust and accountability.

XGBoost (Extreme Gradient Boosting)

A powerful machine learning algorithm known for its high performance in classification and regression tasks. It's widely used in data science competitions and predictive modeling.

XML (Extensible Markup Language)

A structured text format used to store and share data between systems. AI applications use XML for configuration, annotations, and data exchange.

XOR Problem

A classic logic problem that early neural networks struggled to solve. It led to the development of multilayer neural networks capable of learning non-linear relationships.

Letter Y

YAML (YAML Ain't Markup Language)

A human-readable data format often used for AI configuration files, datasets, and machine learning pipelines. It's easy to read and integrates well with Python-based AI frameworks.

Yield Prediction AI

AI systems that forecast agricultural output based on environmental data, crop type, and soil conditions. It supports smarter farming and food sustainability.

Yearly Seasonality Model

A model used in time-series forecasting that accounts for repeating annual patterns — such as sales spikes or weather cycles — to improve accuracy.

YOLO (You Only Look Once)

A fast real-time object detection algorithm that identifies and locates multiple objects in a single pass. It's widely used in autonomous vehicles and security systems.

Letter Z

Zero-Shot Learning

An AI method that allows a model to recognize new objects or tasks it has never seen before by using prior knowledge or contextual reasoning.

Zettabyte

A unit of digital storage equal to one sextillion (10^{21}) bytes. AI models and data centers increasingly operate with zettabyte-scale data due to massive global information growth.

Z-Score Normalization

A statistical technique used to standardize data by subtracting the mean and dividing by the standard deviation. It helps machine learning models handle data with different scales.

Zone-Based AI

A decision-making approach where an AI system divides its environment into regions or "zones" for localized reasoning and optimized control — used in robotics and traffic management.

"Learn AI. Understand AI. Shape the Future."
— Susie Hala

:

Teacher's Overview

THE AI SENSOR ECOSYSTEM

How Artificial Intelligence Sees, Understands, and Connects the World

Purpose of This Book

Artificial intelligence cannot understand the world without information. Every AI system depends on sensors that collect data from its surroundings. This book introduces students to the technologies that allow intelligent systems to see, hear, detect movement, measure environmental conditions, recognize speech, identify objects, and interact safely with people and the physical world. Students learn that sensors are the bridge between the digital and physical worlds, making them one of the most important foundations of modern artificial intelligence.

Learning Goals

By the end of this book, students should be able to:

- Explain what sensors are and why AI systems depend on them.
- Describe the different types of sensors used in artificial intelligence.
- Understand how sensor data becomes useful information for AI models.
- Recognize the relationship between sensors, machine learning, and decision-making.
- Compare human senses with artificial sensing technologies.
- Explain how AI uses multiple sensors together to improve accuracy.
- Discuss ethical issues involving privacy, surveillance, and responsible sensor use.
- Identify real-world applications of AI sensors in transportation, healthcare, education, manufacturing, agriculture, robotics, and smart cities.
- Evaluate the benefits and limitations of sensor technologies.
- Understand how sensor ecosystems will continue to evolve alongside future AI systems.

Big Ideas

Students should leave this book understanding several key concepts:

- AI cannot perceive the world without data.
- Sensors are the "eyes, ears, and nervous system" of intelligent machines.
- Different sensors collect different kinds of information.
- Combining multiple sensors often produces more reliable results.
- Better data usually leads to better AI decisions.
- Human judgment remains essential when interpreting AI outputs.
- Responsible sensor use requires attention to privacy, ethics, fairness, and security.

Suggested Classroom Discussion Questions

Teachers may use questions such as:

- How is a camera similar to a human eye?
- Why would a self-driving vehicle need more than one type of sensor?
- What problems might occur if sensors collect incorrect information?
- How do AI systems determine which sensor information is most important?
- What responsibilities do governments and companies have when deploying sensor technologies?
- Where do students interact with AI sensors in their daily lives?

Cross-Curricular Connections

This book supports learning across multiple subject areas.

Computer Science

- Artificial intelligence
- Machine learning
- Robotics
- Computer vision
- Data collection

Science

- Human sensory systems
- Physics of light, sound, and motion
- Environmental monitoring

Engineering

- Robotics
- Automation
- Embedded systems
- Internet of Things (IoT)

Mathematics

- Measurement
- Data interpretation
- Pattern recognition
- Probability

Digital Citizenship

- Privacy
- Cybersecurity
- Ethical technology use
- Responsible innovation

Hands-On Extension Activities

Teachers may encourage students to:

- Identify AI sensors used throughout their school or community.
- Compare sensors found in different smartphones.
- Research how hospitals use AI sensors to improve patient care.
- Investigate how autonomous vehicles combine cameras, radar, lidar, GPS, and ultrasonic sensors.
- Design a concept for an AI-powered smart classroom using multiple sensors.

Essential Vocabulary

Students should become familiar with terms such as:

- Sensor
- Input
- Data
- Computer Vision
- LiDAR
- Radar

- GPS
- Accelerometer
- Gyroscope
- Infrared
- Ultrasonic
- IoT
- Machine Learning
- Pattern Recognition
- Sensor Fusion
- Real-Time Processing

Preparing Students for the Future

Artificial intelligence will increasingly depend on networks of intelligent sensors operating in homes, schools, hospitals, factories, farms, vehicles, and cities. Understanding how these technologies work enables students to become informed users, thoughtful innovators, and responsible decision-makers. Rather than viewing sensors as isolated devices, students should recognize them as part of an interconnected ecosystem that allows AI to perceive, interpret, and respond to the world around it.

My recommendation for the entire IntelliGloss AI Education Series

I would create a **standard 2-page Teacher's Guide** that appears in **every one of your books**. The sections could stay consistent, while the examples and learning goals are tailored to each topic. This consistency would make the series feel cohesive and easier for teachers to use.

A standard format might include:

1. Purpose of This Book
2. Learning Objectives
3. Key Vocabulary
4. Essential Questions
5. Cross-Curricular Connections
6. Classroom Activities
7. Assessment Ideas
8. Discussion Prompts
9. Extension Activities
10. Preparing Students for the Future

That approach would give every IntelliGloss AI Education Series book a recognizable teacher resource while keeping each guide specific to the book's subject. I think it would add real value for educators evaluating your series for classroom use.

NOTE:

NOTE:

NOTE:

www.ingramcontent.com/pod-product-compliance
Lightning Source LLC
Chambersburg PA
CBHW041753220926
51847CB00014B/193
* 9 7 8 1 9 7 2 9 2 5 2 2 5 *